STO

11-13-75

BUYING YOUR HOUSE.:

A COMPLETE GUIDE TO

INSPECTION AND EVALUATION

BUYING YOUR HOUSE:

A COMPLETE GUIDE TO

INSPECTION AND EVALUATION

JOSEPH C. DAVIS

and

CLAXTON WALKER

1975

EMERSON BOOKS, INC.

Buchanan, New York 10511

CONTENTS 1882904

Crawl spaces
Insulation in crawl spaces
The attic
The insulation; ventilation in the attic; roof framing; pipes ducts, wires, and chimneys; signs of leaks; attic use; the firewall.

Wood-strip flooring
Parquet Floors
Resilient floors
Carpeting
Surface flammability; surface textures; indoor-outdoor carpeting; how to check carpeting; backing; padding.
Walls and ceilings
The drywall; wet plaster; plaster cracks; special types ceilings and walls; wood panelling; condition of paint; electrical outlets; types of switches; air leakage through walls and floors; wall thermostats; wall insulation.
Doors and windows
Doors; windows.
The bathroom
Leaks in the bathroom; water pressure; the toilet; tubs and shower stalls; wall exposure; make tests in the bathroom.
The kitchen
Kitchen location; convenience and relationship of equipment; cabinets and pantry; think vertically in a kitchen; the refrigerator; range and oven; the exhaust fan; the dishwasher; the garbage disposal; sink faucets.
Household appliances
The washer and dryer; central vacuum systems; appliance warranties.
House floor plan
Bedrooms; the dining room; the family room; the recreation room; foyer.

Electric system
Current availability; voltage; service panel box; branch circuits; aluminum vs. copper wiring; safety device for swimming pool.
The plumbing system
Metal piping; plastic piping; clues to past plumbing

problems; the water hammer; frost closure of stack vents.

Heating systems
The hot-air furnace; hydronic heating; steam heating; electric heating; panel heating system; heating capacities; solar heating; fireplaces.

The hot water heater
Gas-fired hotwater heaters; electric hotwater heaters; deterioration of hotwater heaters; how to inspect and evaluate hotwater heaters.

Air-conditioning
Electric central air-conditioning; problems with electric systems; the central gas-absorption system; comparison of gas system with electric system; the add-on central system; capacities of central system; window units and units installed through the wall.

The heat pump
Problems with air-to-air heat pumps; successful heat pump operation; guarantees for air conditioning and heat pumps.

Evaporative coolers

Schematic Diagram of a Home

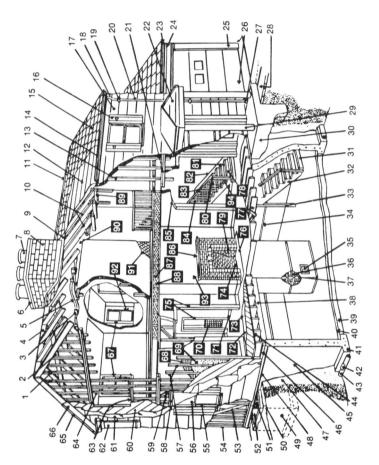

1. Gable stud
2. Collar beam
3. Ceiling joist
4. Ridge board
5. Insulation
6. Chimney cap
7. Chimney flues
8. Chimney
9. Chimney flashing
10. Rafters
11. Ridge
12. Roof boards
13. Stud
14. Eave gutter
15. Roofing
16. Blind or shutter
17. Bevel siding
18. Downspout gooseneck
19. Downspout strap
20. Downspout leader
21. Double plate
22. Entrance canopy
23. Garage cornice
24. Facia

25. Door jamb
26. Garage door
27. Downspout shoe
28. Sidewalk
29. Entrance post
30. Entrance platform
31. Stair riser
32. Stair stringer
33. Girder post
34. Chair rail
35. Cleanout door
36. Furring strips
37. Corner stud
38. Girder
39. Gravel fill
40. Concrete floor
41. Foundation footing
42. Paper strip
43. Drain tile
44. Diagonal subfloor
45. Foundation wall
46. Sill plate
47. Backfill
48. Termite shield

49. Window well wall
50. Grade line
51. Basement sash
52. Window well
53. Corner brace
54. Corner stud
55. Window frame
56. Window light
57. Wall studs
58. Header
59. Window cripple
60. Wall sheathing
61. Building paper
62. Pilaster
63. Rough header
64. Window stud
65. Cornice moulding
66. Facia board
67. Window casing
68. Lath
69. Insulation
70. Wainscoting
71. Baseboard
72. Building paper

73. Finish floor
74. Ash dump
75. Door trim-casing
76. Fireplace hearth
77. Floor joists
78. Stair riser
79. Fire brick
80. Newel cap
81. Stair tread
82. Finish stringer
83. Stair rail
84. Balusters
85. Plaster arch
86. Mantel
87. Floor joists
88. Bridging
89. Lookout
90. Attic space
91. Metal lath
92. Window sash
93. Chimney breast
94. Newel

INTRODUCTION

Buying a house is one of the most significant moves you will make in your lifetime. Yet, in spite of this fact, many houses are bought on first impression or on the word of an almost unknown salesperson; too often a prospective buyer, intimidated and overwhelmed, is afraid to turn on the gas range or flush the toilet. Buyers become caught up with what real estate dealers call the "cosmetic" effect — looks, neighborhood, carpeting, attractive powder rooms — and ignore the more salient features — good insulation, efficient heating systems, solid structures.

This book is written for the prospective home buyer who wants to go beyond the "cosmetic" level. Its purpose is to save you money and to help you avoid serious defects and such pitfalls of buying as confrontations with builders, previous owners, or manufacturers of appliances conveyed with the property.

The most important lesson this book will teach you is how to inspect a house. In the inspection of a house the buyer should follow a pattern. Start outside and note the shrubbery, trees, garage, patio, roof, paint job and visible construction. Second, go into the basement (or mechanical room), third, the attic, and finally, make a general survey of the interior rooms. Try to relate your indoor examination to outside indicators; for example, if the lawn slopes toward the house look out for a leaky basement.

Careful inspection and technical evaluation of a house should play a more important role than emotional impact. Remember, you may be living in the house long after the impact has vanished. A good second-hand house may turn you off on first impression: screens may be pushed in, shutters sagging, and the garden overgrown with weeds. However, these are actually quite minor; you may be getting a bargain — a real diamond in the rough.

In order to make an adequate inspection of the house, the buyer must have a firm grasp of the basic construction techniques. Most of the techniques and practices described here are conventional; the building and appliance industry is changing so fast that it would be impossible to include information about such housing innovations as steel walls, structures built in standard-sized sections (modules), or new untried foundation techniques. Therefore we have chosen to cover only those items which have been on the scene some years and have proven themselves to be practical and durable.

Some important non-technical information related to buying a house is also included. Forewarnings and hints about warrantees and guarantees on furnaces, water heaters, air-conditioners, and other appliances are given, and an entire chapter is devoted to the enlightened household warranty plans that have appeared on the scene in the past few years.

Since ease of maintenance is an important factor to consider in buying a house, a number of maintenance hints are included in the text.

At the end of the book, a glossary of technical terms is provided to help unravel any confusion the reader might have with the technical information presented.

Read this book carefully before beginning your first inspection. Refer to it after each subsequent inspection. You cannot learn the technical aspects of buying a house all at once, nor will this book be of any value if you don't apply what you read. Like learning algebra or cooking, it takes time and practice. At the end of a few weeks or a few houses, you will be surprised how well you have learned to judge. This will be of inestimable value, not only in buying but also in maintaining your new home.

These recommendations and home-buying hints will help you to make a careful evaluation of any house to see if it's the right one for you.

Of course, no house — new or secondhand — will pass the test of careful scrutiny on all points. A trade-off between technical perfection and other features such as architectural appeal, neighborhood, cost and intuitive feelings about a house will play a large part in your decision.

It becomes even harder to find the perfect house when you consider the problems created by our mobile society. You may move from a community of charming old homes on wide tree-lined streets to a community that offers mostly treeless split level tract homes. This may be hard to accept, but you can take solace in the fact that tract houses provide more living space, and more amenities like extra bathrooms, larger kitchens, air-conditioning, updated tile, and high ceilinged basements.

We want to make you a knowledgeable home buyer. If you can assess the defects in a house you like and feel will have good resale value, it often pays to buy it. Your family will have the fun of remodelling and gardening, while you gain a tax deduction and build up equity to buy a better house later.

Compared to housing of the past, our mass housing is not bad. Yet, even so, we must remain vigilant in our efforts to demand and obtain better quality in mass housing. We must not let the charlatans, shortcutters, and fastsellers get away with anything.

1. FIRST IMPRESSIONS

When you leave your car and walk up to a house, the first thing you will notice is its general appearance — the style, lawn, shrubs, sidewalks and paint job. You may be impressed. Or you may not.

Your first impression should influence your decision to buy for two reasons. First, of course, we all want to put our best foot forward, to look well and prosperous. Second, "first impression" will affect its resale value, an important consideration.

Landscaping. A good landscaping job is important for these same two reasons: personal satisfaction and resale value. The essential factors in landscaping are trees, lawns, shrubs, and drainage.

Trees offer beauty and shade, and provide homes for songbirds. Shady trees reduce air-conditioning costs, and large trees make for an established community appearance.

However, before you let your first impression carry you away entirely, look at the shrubs and trees carefully. Have they been well nurtured and pruned? Are some of the trees showing evidence of decay and dying? In old homes be on the lookout for trees with black ants swarming around their bases, a sign of internal rotting; if nothing is done soon, those trees are not long for this earth. It might be better to have no trees or shrubs at all rather than sick, scraggly, overgrown ones that will have to be cut down later at your expense — and trees are expensive to remove.

17

A large tree on the south or southwest side will make the house more comfortable in summer. If buying a new house, this is where the biggest tree should be planted and as soon as possible. A growing tree is an investment which increases in value each year.

Oak, maple, pine and palms are all fine trees for residential planting, if suitable to your climate. Before selecting a tree, check with a good nursery for undesirable features. The fast-growing Chinese chestnut, for instance, drops bushels of flower-like tassels in the Spring.

If you are considering a new house and there are trees there, expect some of them to die. Trees often die during project development since construction may change the level of the water table or increase the exposure of the trees. When inspecting note the condition of leaves and twigs. In summer a sick tree will be dropping leaves prematurely and have sparse underdeveloped growth; in winter the absence of new small, twig growth may indicate an unhealthy tree.

Shrubs rather than trees are most important in foundation planting. The foundations of a house should be hidden by evergreen shrubs — arborvitae, hollies, etc. Unfortunately, most

Fig. 1a. Tall shrubs and trees cover windows and detract from architectural individuality.

newer homes lack plantings large enough to relate the house to the earth and, conversely, older homes tend toward overgrowth. How many 20-50 year old homes have you seen where the "foundation planting" is now thin at the foundation but tall or taller than the roof, covering windows, entrance, railings, etc.? Generally speaking, shrubs should be kept about window-sill height, except at the corners where taller conical-shaped bushes should be 1/2 to 3/4 of the height of the roof line; this softens the house corners. Tall corner bushes should be followed by smaller globular and flat varieties, particularly in high, square houses. (See Fig. 1.)

Striking azaleas, forsythia, lilacs and hydrangeas in front of a house all contribute to first impression and to resale value. In the far southern regions lush low tropical growth with palmetto leaves are inviting.

Fig. 1b. Shrubs at windowsill height give a more pleasing appearance; individuality of architecture is thereby enhanced.

The lawn can add much beauty to a home; a good lawn will catch your eye as you first walk up, and impress others later. However, don't be paranoid about crabgrass or dandelions; a lawn can be cured in three or four years with some attention and not too much money — and of course there are many happy people in the United States living in well-constructed, attractive, tasteful homes, who worry as little about crabgrass as they do about dust in the attic.

If you move into a newly-constructed house before the grading is done and the lawn planted, make sure at the time of closing that money is taken out of your payment and placed in escrow to be released after the grading and planting. New lawns may erode or struggle because little topsoil has been provided by the builder. Make sure there is an understanding about whose responsibility it is to *establish* the lawn. In some areas of the United States it is customary for the builder to furnish sod rather than seed. An advantage here is that some top soil is gained.

Insist on a good planting job; avoid a pure strain of only one type of seed. One of the finest commercial methods of planting grass seed today is to squirt a mixture of seed, mulch, and fertilizer under pressure onto the graded soil; this process is called Hydroseeding. It yields a fine lawn, almost as perfect as those pictured in the advertisements for weed-killers and lawn appliances!

Good yard drainage is also an essential factor in landscaping. Check the area around the foundation and outward for a distance of about six feet. A leaky basement, a sagging stoop, or sinking foundations could result if the terrain slopes downward toward the house. The land in that critical six feet should slope downward *away* from the house at least six inches. This is most important on new houses, since the landfill will settle. However, if there is not sufficient slope, one or two truck loads of earth-fill can be used for fill-in; the price is usually reasonable.

Look, too, for serious sinking of the lawn due to a subterranean stream. This correction may require many wheelbarrows of dirt for filling. A four or five foot area with a three inch depression would be suspicious. The likelihood of such a serious sinking condition is remote, but it would be wise to ask the neighbors if the house was built over a stream or drain bed. In time, you can recognize this condition by observing the general terrain and earth-fill. Large, old trees for example, will not exist in areas covered by fill.

In some areas of the country, particularly in California, houses have been built on land subject to sinking and landslide. Here again judicious inquiry of the neighbors and local-government engineers will help. In some areas the trouble stems from a particular type of soil known as bentonite or montmorillonite. When this occurs, entire neighborhoods are affected and sinking foundations are common.

Observe the terrain of the entire neighborhood with respect to water drainage. When the house is at the bottom of a hill or in a valley, ask the neighbors if they are having problems with leaky basements. If the water table is high, an expensive sump pump system in the basement will be required to remove water after a heavy rain.

Exterior Paint. A well-painted house with harmonious coloring will attract you, while a shabbily painted exterior may turn you off — and rightfully so. Flaking and peeling may be due to a number of causes, including inferior paint, poor painting techniques, excess moisture in the house, and air pollution. If there is flaking paint over brick masonry, probably latex paint was used over chalky surface; either the chalk should have been cleaned off entirely or oil-base paint used instead of latex. Also, some hardburned brick will simply never hold paint. If the flaking is on galvanized steel gutters and downspouts, they were undoubtedly painted without a proper undercoat. (See Chapter 10.)

Paints with excessive chalk, when dried, will soon rub off on hands and clothing. Look for this chalking problem on doors and fences. Excessive paint-peel may also be an alert for excess water vapor within the house; keep this in mind for your inspection of the basement and possible water problems.

Stains and efflorescence. It is common to see unsightly white stains from cheap, chalky paint, seeping down from windowsills on to the brickwork below. Such stains are difficult to remove but can be cleaned with a dilute solution of muriatic acid and a

21

lot of elbow grease. Consult a quality paint store about this. They may be able to advise you on how to mix a tinting material with a color that matches the brickwork, so you can cover those parts that cannot be cleaned.

Another common detraction to a house's appearance is efflorescence, a chemical action on the brickwork. This ugly whitish encrustation is extremely difficult to remove; you can do so only by applying a dilute solution of muriatic acid. Directions must be scrupulously followed. (See Chapter 10.) Efflorescence is more prevalent and occurs with greater intensity if bricks get wet before they are laid. Builders should therefore keep them covered at the construction site.

ARCHITECTURAL STYLES

Many architectural styles are found in this country. Some of the principal ones are illustrated and described on the pages that follow. In actual construction, of course, most houses reflect individual tastes, adaptations to project and economic limitations, and also to climatic conditions; in reality, there are few "pure" styles.

Fig. 2. Two Story Colonial or Traditional. Since Colonial times most frequently reproduced style in America. It ranges from the simple project-built unit to the detailed, and authentically crafted house.
Courtesy of American Technical Society

22

Fig. 3. Garrison Colonial. This ever popular Colonial style derives its name from the early Colonial defense garrison. The upper story projects and overhangs the lower level.

Fig. 4. Georgian Colonial. An early eastern Colonial style. Very formal when adapted to larger houses. Still very popular and reproduced in nearly every community of the midwestern, eastern and southeastern states.

23

Fig. 5. Southern Colonial. Developed in the south as one of our earliest colonial forms. The large two-story portico offered shade from the hot southern sun.

Fig. 6. French Provincial. Originated in France in the 17th century. Usually built in this country as a custom designed house. It's typified by its mansard roof, symmetrical features, and casement windows.

Fig. 7. American Gothic. This was the low cost house that lined the streets of many small towns. A product of the industrial revolution that brought many working people from the farms to the towns. A house also built by small farmers. Its construction often made use of a single span joist, bearing on front and rear walls only, with no middle support.

Courtesy of Prentice Hall, Inc.

Fig. 8. Split Level. A descriptive name for its basic construction. Several half flights of stairs split the floor plan into three to five levels. May be styled as colonial or contemporary. Seen since 1950 in all sections of the country.

25

Fig. 9. Rambler or Ranch. A one-story house in either the traditional or contemporary style. It is actually an elongation of the bungalow house of the early 1900's.

Courtesy of North American Housing Corporation.

Fig. 10. Bungalow. A small, one-story house that lent itself to additions and style changes. A familiar sight in suburban and city areas across the country. Mass-produced from 1910 to 1930; seldom since duplicated.

Fig. 11. Dutch Colonial. A very popular colonial style in the eastern states. Its gambrel roof with dormers is its most distinguishing characteristic. Usually has a center hall floor plan. Built by the Pennsylvania Dutch, the roofline is similar to their barns.

Fig. 12. Cape Cod. One of the earliest northeastern colonials. Mass-produced following World War I and continuing through World War II. It is still popular. Center entrance, bedrooms on first floor. Often sold now with an unfinished expandable attic. This house has taken on many forms; sometimes quite large with porches, wings and large shed dormers.

Fig. 13. Salt Box. A New England colonial design. Not copied much in the last century. The unique roofline resembled the old country-store salt box. When possible, the long sloped roof was oriented toward the prevailing winter winds. The long slope of the roof is adaptable, with southern orientation, as a solar collector for harnessing sunlight.

Fig. 14. New Orleans Style. A symmetrical, ornate, two and three story, post Revolutionary War style, with much French and Spanish influence. The ornate ironwork and balconies were adapted to a myriad of similar styles and also to geographical areas all over the southern and Middle Atlantic states. The expense of its ornateness eventually led to its decline.

28

Fig. 15. Spanish Mission House. A far Western and Southwestern style used for private homes since the early 1800's.

Fig. 16. Monterey. One of the first widely built two-story houses in the west. Built of local adobe brick with an overlay of plaster.

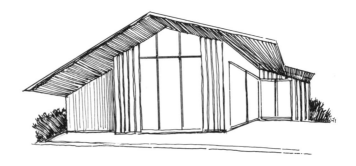

Fig. 17. Contemporary. A modern style of architecture incorporating wide expanses of glass and a low pitched roof with wide overhangs. Usually one-story and often has exposed structural members with no ornamentation.

Fig. 18. Modern House. Much talked about in Frank Lloyd Wright's heyday as the future style of residential architecture.

30

Fig. 19. Row House. The old row house is common to nearly every large city in America, particularly in the East. Often of federal styling. Built in large numbers from the late 1800's to the 1930's. Because each unit shares at least one wall with the next, heating and cooling costs are lessened and maintenance is lower.

Fig. 20a. Town-house. (Western-Spanish architecture): A row house adapted to individuality and past tradition of the locale. Seen in Western cities.

31

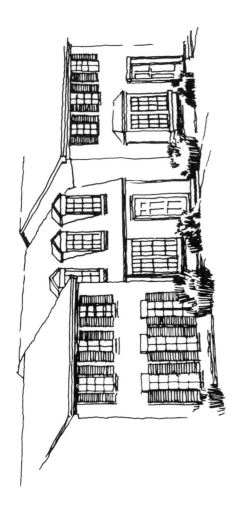

Fig. 20b. Town-houses. A more recent name for row houses. Town-houses are more individually styled. Connected together, they eliminate side yard and wide lots. Heating and cooling costs are cut because of common walls. An answer to high, in-town land cost. Those pictured are of colonial design, but contemporary town-houses are gaining in popularity.

The ten illustrations above are based upon architectural style from © copyright 1973 HOUSES: The Illustrated Guide to Construction Design and Systems with permission of the National Institute of Real Estate Brokers. All rights reserved. For further explanation of these and 47 other architectural sytles, write NIREB, 155 East Superior Street, Chicago 60611.

Fig. 21. English Tudor. Distinguished by its steep roofs, gables, and half-timber exposed decorative framing — often set in stucco. Steel casement type windows, usually without shutters.   Courtesy of American Technical Society

TABLE 1

SEASONAL HEAT GAIN FACTORS FOR DOUBLE STRENGTH (1/8 in.) SHEET GLASS PLACED VERTICALLY IN HOUSES: RELATED TO SOLAR POSITION IN FOUR SELECTED NORTHERN LATITUDES (Data For One Day Per Month During Winter And Summer Season)

BTU PER HOUR PER SQUARE FOOT OF GLASS

TIME OF YEAR	TIME OF DAY	24 Degrees — Approx. latitude for: Miami, Fla. Monterey, Mex.					32 Degrees — Approx. latitude for: Fort Worth, Tex. Jacksonville, Fla. San Diego, Cal.					40 Degrees — Approx. latitude for: Denver, Colo. Indianapolis, Ind. Philadelphia, Pa.					48 Degrees — Approx. latitude for: Minot, N.D. Quebec, Can. Seattle, Wash.				
		W	**SW**	**S**	**SE**	**E**	**W**	**SW**	**S**	**SE**	**E**	**W**	**SW**	**S**	**SE**	**E**	**W**	**SW**	**S**	**SE**	**E**
WINTER (NOV. DEC. JAN. FEB.)	A.M.	382	928	3202	4224	2727	318	1020	3278	3967	2281	252	1061	3207	3653	1905	181	1012	2821	3011	1384
	P.M.	2727	4224	3202	928	382	2281	3967	3278	1020	318	1905	3653	3207	1061	252	1384	3011	2821	1012	181
	TOTAL	**3109**	**5152**	**6404**	**5152**	**3109**	**2599**	**4987**	**6556**	**4987**	**2599**	**2157**	**4714**	**6414**	**4714**	**2157**	**1565**	**4023**	**5642**	**4023**	**1565**
SUMMER (JUNE, JULY, AUG.)	A.M.	510	523	615	1884	2785	515	550	816	2254	2865	512	596	1129	2621	2941	508	673	1490	2970	3069
	P.M.	2785	1884	615	523	510	2865	2254	816	550	515	2941	2621	1129	596	512	3069	2970	1490	673	508
	TOTAL	**3295**	**2407**	**1230**	**2407**	**3295**	**3380**	**2804**	**1632**	**2804**	**3380**	**3453**	**3217**	**2258**	**3217**	**3453**	**3577**	**3643**	**2980**	**3643**	**3577**
BEST ORIENTATION FOR YEAR ROUND BENEFIT			√	√	√			√	√	√			√	√	√			√	√	√	

Data obtained from Handbook of Fundamentals, 1972, American Society of Heating, Refrigerating and Air-Conditioning Engineers.

34

THE BEST ORIENTATION FOR YOUR HOUSE

Consider three factors in the orientation of a house:
1. Sunlight
2. Prevailing winds   **1882904**
3. View and setting

Of course, we are setting forth the ideal here — there is no perfect orientation for sunlight since the sun moves, and no perfect orientation for prevailing winds, since winds do not always come from the same direction. And, of course, one rarely finds the perfect view. Your final choice of a house should be one which offers a compromise among these three factors, with an emphasis on that factor which is your own personal preference.

Sunlight. Orientation for sunlight varies considerably with latitude. In Miami (26 degrees), the windows of a house facing due west and due east get about as much sunlight during the winter months as during the summer months. In the same latitude, windows facing southwest, south, or southeast receive much more sunlight in the winter than in the summer — a much better orientation.

Table 1 points out the most favorable window orientations in latitudes ranging from 26 degrees (Miami) to 48 degrees (Quebec, Canada). From the table, determine if the house you are considering will be easy to heat. Heat gain is the amount of heat gained in one square foot of 1/8 inch sheet glass during one hour. Heat gain is obviously directly related to the amount of sunlight received.

In using the table, note the total heat gain values (shown in bold type) and compare them for winter and summer. The best year-round orientation is indicated by a check mark in the lowest row of figures; best orientations are those which give the most heat in winter and the least in summer. Although there are data for four winter months and only three summer months, the difference has little effect on orientation comparison.

There are other considerations which depend on your family. For example, northern light is valuable for work areas because it is consistent and offers no glare. Children's bedrooms might have a southern exposure to give them as much sunlight as possible. Perhaps one member of the family dislikes a sunlit room early in the morning because it disturbs his or her sleep.

Since fuel economy is important these days, note how large window areas in a house relate to the prevailing wind; a window-wall that faces into the path of a prevailing, harsh wind will be expensive to heat. The Weather Bureau in your area (National Weather Service, National Oceanic and Atmospheric Administration, Department of Commerce) can tell you about local prevailing winds.

In regard to view, take advantage of parks, trees, or obvious vistas such as distant mountains and lakes. In the city, keep in mind that future development may obstruct the view, or a neighbor may pile his garbage cans opposite your large window.

CONSIDER THE COMMUNITY AND NEIGHBORHOOD

Among the more important neighborhood factors are:
- Convenience to shopping and work.
- Quality of schools and convenience to them.
- Local covenants and restrictions.
- State and local taxes.
- Assessments; Sewer, street and other front-foot charges.
- Streets, safety, traffic, parking, noise.
- Appearance of neighboring houses, including back yards. Are the houses improved or neglected?
- Trees and landscaping.
- Social and economic compatibility.

You should also consider proximity to large building developments and parking areas. A house near a planned subway stop may lose value and environmental quality due to increased air-pollution — or it may gain in value and you can profit on re-sale. Beware of localities near an offending electric generating plant, chemical plant, incinerator or other sources of heavy air or noise pollution.

If you are moving into a new community, investigate the water supply. Because of chemical pollution and lack of virus protection, some city supplies are approaching a level where radical reassessment is needed. For more information on this, read Consumer Reports for June, July and August of 1974.

How does this house stack up with the neighborhood? Compare the relative appearance of the house (and price) to others in the neighborhood. It may be a better investment to buy a modest house in an expensive neighborhood of large houses than an expensive larger house in a run-down neighborhood. However, while it may be a better investment, you will have *less house* and *less living space* at greater expense. Small houses in an expensive neighborhood gain value from the neighborhood and are assessed accordingly.

Architectural appeal is a matter of preference. The house you are considering may appeal to you—something you have been looking for all your life. Yet, it may register a complete zero for others—even incur hostility from the neighbors if too unorthodox. The more your preference deviates from the norm, the fewer buyers you will have at resale time.

Resale potential. For resale purposes it is important that you know which styles endure in popularity in your geographical area. For example, the two-story colonial is an old style but it is still the nation's best seller. Ranch houses in the western states and Spanish style houses in California are two other examples. Houses, like men's and women's clothes, have fashions. It is wise to understand present and possible future fashion to judge its effect on demand in years to come. If you really want an oddball house, buy it; but understand if the price is below the market now, it will probably be on the low end of the market when you sell.

Is there flood danger? Flooding occurs not only in rural areas but also in cities. Inquire about this before you buy. Someone may be trying to unload a house that was seriously flooded before, or may be in the future if the area is vulnerable and lacks flood control measures.

2. AN OVERVIEW OF THE OUTSIDE

In legal jargon, the structures apart from the house are called its appurtenances; you will find the word on your deed. The major appurtenances are garages, walks, patios, retaining walls, fences, stairwells, and dry wells.

The Garage. Garages can be either detached or attached, and of course there are advantages and disadvantages to both types. The detached garage comes with most older houses, while the attached one is the most popular today.

Detached garages. The detached garage is usually small and can only accommodate a compact car. However, it may be used to store lawn furniture, mowers, tools, and the kind of "contraption junk" the average housewife doesn't want around the house.

Watch out for mildew under the roof deck and on the studs of older detached garages. This is evidence of a leaky roof and calls for inspection of the shingles. Shingling a defective roof is described in Chapter 3; rolled roofing is not recommended because it lacks durability. Once the roof is waterproof, mildew can be washed away with a 5 percent solution of sodium hypochlorite (common household bleach), followed by a rinsing of clear water.

The next step in your inspection is opening and closing the garage door. The older type of door that swings out generally will be rotting or dragging but can be replaced by the newer overhead type. This can be accomplished at a reasonable cost provided there is at least seven feet of room floor to ceiling. However, many old frame detached garages are not worth the expense of improvement.

For proper water runoff the detached garage should have gutters or at least a wide overhang. If it has neither, look carefully for evidence of rotting of the outside wall bottoms. A final thing to watch out for in these garages is termites. (See Chapter 3.)

The attached garage requires many safety features which detached structures do not. In some states, the ceiling and wall connecting garage and house must be plaster, masonry, or other fire-retardant material; the door from garage to house must be solid wood or covered with sheet metal.

On the negative side, carbon monoxide fumes can be a threat in an attached garage. These fumes are heavier than air and will slide into a basement if the garage is on the same level or higher that the basement. Most codes require a four-inch step down from house to garage. A curb is a partial remedy; if you buy a house with an attached garage, realize that the problem will always be with you. The dangerous exhaust fumes can get into any adjacent room if the car is allowed to run with the outer garage door closed.

Sometimes water will seep in between the house and attached garage if proper flashing between the roof and the wall of the house is not provided. In either type—detached or attached—look for a proper slope so the floor can be hosed out easily, melted clumps of snow dripping from the car should run off.

A minimum of four inches of insulation (R-13) should be placed between the joists above the attached garage ceiling, if there is heated living space above. The reflective insulation (or vapor barrier) should be on the warm side with the fibrous material below. Detailed information on R designations for insulation—R-5 to R-19—is given in Glossary.

Driveways which slope downward offer potential trouble in both types of garages. Drains get stopped up and, after a good down-pour, flooding results. If there is no drain, beware! Also watch out for driveways that tilt sideways toward a house: you may very well wind up with a leaky basement. A flat driveway, or one that slopes gently toward the street, is your best bet.

Of the two solid types of driveway—concrete and asphalt—concrete is better, because it has intrinsic strength that blacktop lacks. If you are building a new house, or have some option when a house is being built, insist on at least four—but preferably six-inch concrete with wire mesh reinforcement.

Asphalt, on the other hand, is a pliable material, and durability and strength depend on the firmness of the base underneath; good blacktop driveways may have only two inches of blacktop on a good solid-packed gravel base. However, if the asphalt appears to be giving or cracking, it is impossible to build up strength by adding more blacktop.

There is nothing wrong with a gravel or bluestone driveway. It can be attractive, especially with a country home; if it is on a solid base and thick enough (at least three inches), it can be blacktopped later. A steep driveway would not work for gravel or bluestone; the flatter the better.

Finally, make sure that your driveway is at least nine feet wide. It is also convenient to have a large turn-around area for your car, but do not expect to find this in most older houses.

Walks and patios. In a newly-constructed house, the less concrete work, slabs, or masonry in the yard, the better off you are; they will settle and often crack or tilt. Root growth will break up sidewalks and patios poured or constructed near a large tree. Repair of concrete is temporary unless a near-complete replacement is undertaken, whereas flagstone or bricks laid on sand or earth can easily be lifted and repaired.

Bricks in patios and concrete slabs usually sink if applied directly over backfill. If they develop a general slope toward the house, water may leak into the basement; this is common in new houses where the backfill has not yet settled.

Retaining walls are designed to hold back the earth in sloping lots and terraces. Most are built improperly — too thin and with improper backfill — and many are crooked or leaning from the pressure of wet or frozen earth.

A properly made mortar-jointed wall should be one foot thick for every three feet in height and should be on a wide footing below frost level. Dry-stone walls should be even thicker, but no footing is required below frost level. Hollow cinder block alone is not practical, but when rods and concrete are placed in the cavities, a strong wall results. All walls should be backfilled with gravel, and weep holes should be provided to reduce frost heave and to let water seep through.

Basement stairwells. An improperly drained basement stairwell can cause flooding. Ascertain if the drain is operative, and if it leads to a storm sewer. In some areas of the U.S., the drain leads only to a hole, or small "dry-well," which can fill up and overflow quickly in a heavy rain.

Such small dry-wells are being used more and more in suburbia to relieve the heavy load on sanitary and storm drain systems. The stairwell area-way should be lower than the basement floor to prevent direct flow into the basement; six inch sill is standard. A built-up dam (curb) could be erected as a partial remedy.

Dry wells in yard. You may discover a much larger dry-well in the back yard of the house you are inspecting — a deep hole filled with gravel for water drain-off from the downspouts. It really amounts to a reservoir for water to collect in before it can run down into the ground. Some builders or homeowners construct a retention tank for this purpose; the tank consists of a large corrugated steel pipe vertically sunk into a hole lined with gravel. These drywells must be located at least fifteen feet away from the house — even further if possible — to prevent water pressure build-up from working back toward the basement.

3. LOOKING AT THE
EXTERIOR CONSTRUCTION

After scrutinizing the appurtenances of a prospective house, turn to the structure of the house itself. The first step in this is the exterior examination, in which you should check the roofing, foundations, wall structures, windows, doors, porches and stoops, and possible insect infestation.

THE ROOF

The first thing to observe on your exterior examination is the roof. Look for missing or aging shingles, and sagging or loose flashing.

Several general rules for inspecting and judging roofs are:
- A steep-pitched roof rarely leaks, but is more difficult to repair than a low pitch roof.
- Simplicity of roof-line means lower maintenance cost and less tendency to leak. Fewer dormers and valleys help in this respect. Gutters on one-story houses can be easily cleaned.
- An overhang helps window and sidewall protection and reduces cooling costs.
- Roofs exposed to the south (in the northern hemisphere) deteriorate more rapidly.
- The life of a roof does not vary too much from the life of the material from which it is made; deterioration rates will be the same.

- Final judgment on a roof should be made after inspecting the attic and upstairs ceiling.
- Large trees over brittle shingles (cement or slate) promote breakage and leaf-cleaning chores.

TYPES OF ROOFING

Asphalt shingle roofs. Most roofs today are made of asphalt shingles. These durable shingles have a life-expectancy of fifteen to twenty-five years. They are made of heavy paper, known as felt, which is coated with hot, liquid asphalt, and covered with fine rock granules. The quality is determined by weight per "square" — (100 square feet of applied roof area). Standard asphalt shingles weigh about 235 pounds per square and last up to eighteen years in average climates. Shingles of heavier weight—275 to 325 pounds per square—use thicker felt and more asphalt, and are designed to last up to twenty-five years in average climates.

A good asphalt shingle roof must give protection against high winds. To offer this protection, "self-sealing" shingles are now available. When warmed by the sun soon after application, adhesive seals each shingle to the one above it. These self-sealing jobs of 235-pound grade come on many new houses and are particularly good on the modern, low pitch roofs.

The primary purpose of the granules on the surface of the shingle is to keep the sun off the asphalt. In time, due to exposure to weather and the sun, the granules will wear off. As a result, the sun begins to pock-mark, blister, and make holes in the shingles.

Observe the shingles at close range or use binoculars and look out the window, or climb a ladder. Look for loss of granules or blistering, especially below the slots between the shingle. If you find upon examination that only a few granules are left at this spot, a new roof will be needed within a year or so. If only a few granules are left on the overall shingle, and many have ended up in the gutter or at the bottom of drain spouts, a new roof is needed at once.

Figure 22. A prospective buyer can use binoculars to inspect condition of shingles.

Repair of an asphalt shingle roof is simple and replacement is not too expensive if a contractor places the new shingles over the old ones. However, because of weight consideration, this can usually be done only twice. The roof will get lumpy on a third application, and some codes do not allow this. Look at the gable shingle edges to determine how many times the roof has been reshingled. It is also important to inspect the rafters and roof decking in the attic for dry rot.

Roofs of natural slate. Roofs made of slate shingles add to the value of a house. These shingles are attractive and, if cut from a

45

good mineral bed, will last for a hundred years or more. But watch out for slate that comes from the wrong kind of bed; it will last less than ten years, showing discoloration, separation of the layers, and corners that are beginning to shale off. Fortunately, slate shingles take a long time to die, though; they can show signs of deterioration and still be good for another seven to ten years.

Slate shingles have a higher maintenance cost than asphalt shingles. Each year a few are lost to the freeze-thaw action and because of falling tree limbs. Single ones can be replaced by a professional.

It is sometimes difficult for the prospective buyer to evaluate slate. To help in this situation keep in mind the age in relation to the life expectancy of the roof, and be concerned with the south side of the roof where wear first occurs. Watch out for shingles of a brown color with whitish rings similar to water stains; this is an indication of serious problems and short life. Vermont shingles are generally of good grade and the few brown ones in the roof are usually no cause for alarm. Avoid slate on all low-pitched roofs.

Asbestos cement-shingle roofs. Asbestos shingles, made of Portland cement and asbestos fiber, resemble slate shingles, but are thinner. They are a compromise between asphalt shingles and slate with the added advantage of high fire resistance. Asbestos shingles are brittle, but if not walked on or hit by falling tree limbs may last forty years. However, the cheaper grades, consisting mostly of cement and with only a few asbestos fibers, may not last as long as a good grade of asphalt shingle; repairs can be difficult on these. Asbestos cement material is also used for siding.

Tile roofs. Tile roofing, best suited for warm areas, is most common in California or Florida. Tile roofs are apt to be expensive in other areas. Tiles are heavy, durable, and should be applied on a steep slope to avoid water back-up and leaky roofs. Replacement and repair of these clay products is more difficult than simpler forms of shingles; very few new houses are still using them, and when they are used it is often to impart an architectural flavor.

Roofs with wood shakes and shingles. Hand-split, wood-shake shingles have long been popular in western states, but did not reach the mid-west and east until the late 1960's. Their popularity is due to their texture, deep shadow tones, longevity and compatibility with the colonial tradition.

The shakes are thicker than the sawed-wood shingles common on thirty-five to fifty year old houses. Local codes will sometimes prohibit the use of wood shakes and shingles unless dipped with fire treatment chemicals. Wood-shake shingles should be placed on a roof deck with a reasonably steep slope. Even a pitch of one foot rise for each four feet of horizontal span could cause trouble; the water will work back up the rough joints formed by non-uniformity of thickness and roughness of texture. These shingles can also be used for siding.

Flat roofs. Flat roofs can be either "built-up" or metal. A built-up flat or nearly flat roof must employ a monolithic surface and be independent of the shingle roofs' lap joint surface and rapid water run-off. Due to the flatness and the difficulty in obtaining a completely water-tight and level monolithic surface, puddles of water collect on the rooftop and sometimes seep down into the house. This "ponding" effect can eventually be harmful to both the bituminious built-up and flat metal roofs. Repair is difficult due to the long drying-out time.

Built-up roofs. Built-up roofs consist of alternate layers of felt (a paper-like material) and bitumen (asphalt or tar). The top layer of asphalt or tar is convered with gravel or chips of slag. Premature failure of built-up roofing often originates with initial application. A cold bond is produced when the roofer does not have the manpower to work the hot bitumen fast enough or when his firepots are not adequate; leaks follow. Signs of this are blistering, bubbling looseness, and delamination.

Once built-up roofing has begun leaking, it is difficult to obtain a guaranteed repair. Dumping a can of roof coating or tar where the leak is suspected will sometimes do the trick.

Metal roofs. Standard metal roofs are effective for slopes that are greater than built-up roofing slopes, but do not have a steep enough rise for shingle roofs. With soldered seams, they are effective over flat roof-decks. Often metal roofs are made of steel coated with tin or zinc (galvanized metal). Copper was used with great success on older buildings, but is less frequently used today due to high costs. Longevity in all metal roofs except the copper roofs is largely dependent on protective paint coats.

Because of continual expansion and contraction, a metal roof will sometimes leak at the seams between the overlapping plates; this can usually be cured by application of roofing cement, although a professional soldering job is best if the metal is still in good condition.

Metal was used for steep sloped roofs in the early decades of this century and before. The joints were formed by standing double-folded seams, running in the direction of the slope. New roofs of this type can occasionally be seen today.

Plastic roofs. Plastic roofs have not been on the market long enough to make complete evaluation of their durability and water-shedding qualities. Compared with asphalt shingle roofs, they are expensive.

Gutters and Downspouts

Gutters. Faulty gutters combined with improper grading of the dirt, cause leaky areas around the house, and result in damp or wet basements. Many times these leaky areas are erroneously blamed on underwater springs or high water tables; sometimes, unscrupulous waterproofing companies provide expensive and unnecessary "cures" for a wet basement, when a simple gutter repair or improved grading will do.

Gutters must be large enough to carry the rainwater away before overflow occurs. Five-inch wide gutters are standard and usually suffice; six-inch widths are better for extreme loads.

Copper is the best material used in gutters, lasting forty to fifty years. It is usually unpainted, but since it takes on a brownish color with time, some people have it painted for aesthetic reasons.

To determine for certain that the gutter is copper, scrape off the paint with a knife; if it is, a shiny copper will show where you scraped. Another method is to use a magnet; if the gutter is of galvanized steel, the magnet will be attracted.

Galvanized gutters are common because of lower cost and strength when ladders are placed next to them during leaf-cleaning season. Their normal life, if properly treated and cleaned regularly, is 20 to 25 years. Ailing and leaking gutters can sometimes gain a few more years of service by lining the inside with roof coating or roof cement.

New galvanized gutters should not be painted until a month or two after they have been installed. They should then be covered with a special undercoat, and painted with latex or oil-base paint. It is important that you determine if the aging and undercoating treatment was used by the builder; if not, your gutters may later detract seriously from the appearance of the whole house.

Galvanized steel gutters gained their first significant competitor with the advent of the aluminum gutter in the late 1960's. The paint is baked onto the aluminum gutter beforehand, so the problem of paint-peeling is non-existent. The cheaper of the two grades of aluminum gutters, however, is not as strong as copper or galvanized steel gutters, and can bend and be dented by ladders or falling limbs. The better, stronger grade is more expensive than the galvanized gutters, and does not present this problem.

Occasionally, in old homes in some areas of the country, wood gutters and downspouts are used. They give surprisingly good service.

Plastic gutters came on the market prior to 1960 but never received wide acceptance, principally because of their expense. They are durable and are usually stocked in white only.

Some gutter guards are made of screening to keep the leaves out. These are not entirely effective, but they are particularly helpful for older people who cannot clean the gutters regularly and must pay someone to do the work.

Any gutters under oak or pine trees are subject to more rapid deterioration because of the acidity of the trees. Clean gutters 2 to 3 times a year for longer life.

Some older and even new, contemporary houses do not have gutters and downspouts. Usually no difficulty will occur with these houses if they have wide overhangs and if the soil below these offers good drainage. It is difficult, of course, to grow shrubbery close to these houses.

Finally, watch out for loose gutter spikes; these attach the gutter to the house and, if loose, will cause the gutters to sag and spill water.

Downspouts. Gutters should have sufficient downspouts (or leaders). If the roof is long — forty or more feet — there should be a spout at each end. Normally downspouts have cross sectional dimensions of two by three inches, but a large roof area may require three by four inches. (See description of different types of gutter and downspouts in the Glossary.) The water discharge from the downspouts should land on concrete splash blocks, troughs, or flat stones, and should be directed away from the house. Splash blocks should have a length of three feet or more for run-off.

Downspouts can also lead underground. Underground, running through a pipe, the water will not erode the soil or kill the grass, but may often stop up and require professional help. In northern climates the first section of the pipe often stops up, freezes, and breaks, spilling water onto the adjacent ground and sometimes into the basement. The only way this can be tested is to take your hose and squirt water into the gutter during a dry spell, and watch for dampness on the inside basement wall. If stopped up, the water will bubble up at the spout and underground connections.

Problems with gutter-downspouts. When making the inspection of the gutter-downspout system, look for evidence of gutter overflow on the woodwork below. Watch out for black or dark gray marks caused by leaf and seed stain; this usually means that the gutter-downspout system is not adequate or that bends in the downspouts are too sharp, causing a leaf plug-up.

Look for evidence of improper cleaning of either gutters or downspouts. Leak marks on the inside wall beneath the gutter indicates stopped-up and neglected gutters; leaf clogging at the bend of a downspout can be determined by tapping the downspout at this bend. Look for holes or rust, and for ground-erosion and spill marks on the soil from previous storms.

If the gutters and downspouts are peeling and look like the bark of a shag-bark hickory tree, scrape off the old paint and apply a paint remover. This remover will probably contain methylene chloride, a toxic substance. The job is messy and time-consuming; and it might be better to simply have the gutters replaced. (See Chapter 10.)

Along with the inspection of the water-carry-away system, make sure that the ground slopes away from the walls. If it doesn't, look for evidence of a leaky basement on your indoor inspection. (See Chapter 4.)

Ice dams. In northern areas and in older houses, ice dams, or ridges of ice, can form on the lower and colder parts of the roof, such as the overhang or cornice. This harmful build-up occurs because the rough surface of most shingles provides a sure grip for ice to cling to. It provides a seal so that melting ice and melting snow that runs from the warm area of the roof can no longer travel down and off. Consequently, water backs up under the shingles and goes down into the construction members of the house.

Ice dams are most common in old houses that are not insulated in the attic floor (or between the rafters) and where the upper parts of the roof are relatively warm. The absence of modern roof vents is another contributory factor; without ventilation, the roof top gets warmer and more melting results.

To prevent ice dams on these older houses, two to three feet wide pieces of aluminum flashing are installed at the lower edges of the roof; they replace some lower courses of shingles, and are put under the remaining lower courses and up into the warm area of the roof. With this flashing, water will continue to run down the roof and freeze on the cold area; however as the ice gets thicker, its weight will cause the lower ice to break away and slide down the smooth metal.

Some new houses in cold climates encounter ice dam difficulties even with attic insulation and ventilating louvers; this is the case when the sun melts the snow off a roof which has a southern exposure. During mid-day the water from the melted snow will run freely off the roof. However, as the sun sets and the temperature drops, an ice dam forms as the water from the warmer part of the roof continues to run.

Another way to prevent ice dams is to lay a properly insulated thermal electric wire in the gutter and around the downspout, and plug it into an electric outlet on the exterior wall or through the window. These thermal wires are sold in most home improvement departments of the larger retail chain stores. It's the same sort of wire used in electric blankets.

The older "half-round" gutter that hangs loosely from straps will allow melting ice to overflow behing the gutter, thus preventing formation of a dam. It also avoids ice back-up on the roof, a common problem with the similar "O.G." type gutter which is nailed directly to the house. (See Glossary.)

Snow and Wind Loads

Snowloads. Many new houses in northern areas have serious problems because the roofs are not able to withstand heavy snow loads. Two main reasons account for this: 1) The roof rafters are not of sufficient size and are not braced with collar ties as shown below, and 2) Low roof pitch prevents snow slide-off.

Some newer homes, on the other hand, have a truss type of construction which will carry a tremendous load. They can be built of two by four inch lumber instead of the two by six or two by eight inch lumber commonly used for rafters. The trusses can span a greater distance; spacing can be every two feet on center rather than sixteen or twenty inches on center. There are many types of truss roof rafters, but one of the most common types is the W type. Truss construction, of course, will cut down on attic storage space.

Pitch of the roof and construction details vary according to climate, and local codes will differ. If you are buying a house without truss construction in a northern area, compare the roof pitch and construction with others in your city or county that have successfully withstood snow loads.

Wind loads. Local codes will have special construction requirements if wind loads are heavy in your area. It has been found, as a result of years of observation and tests, that the force exerted by the wind varies from fifteen lbs. per square foot for a roof of fifteen degrees pitch up to thirty-five lbs. for a roof of forty-five degrees pitch. If the roof of a house you are inspecting has a roof with a forty-five degree pitch and wind loads are high, you should check roof construction against local codes. "Hurricane ties" or anchor bolts to prevent lifting may be observable from the attic.

THE FOUNDATION

Footings. Footings or footers are the bases under foundation walls; they are placed below the frost line and rest on solid, undisturbed soil. Footings are usually made of concrete, and are spread over a large surface area to distribute widely the weight of the structure above.

Foundation walls. Foundation walls are usually made of poured concrete or concrete blocks (cinder blocks). Poured concrete walls are stronger because they are strengthened by reinforcing rods, and do not require as much thickness to hold back the dirt fill. An eight-inch wall, properly done, will withstand eight feet of fill against it. Concrete cinder blocks, on the other hand, must have a twelve-inch thickness any time there is over five feet of fill against the wall.

When a basement is involved, waterproofing on the outside is very important. Poured concrete walls, as a rule, do not need parging (an application of 1/2 to 3/4 inch coat of waterproofing

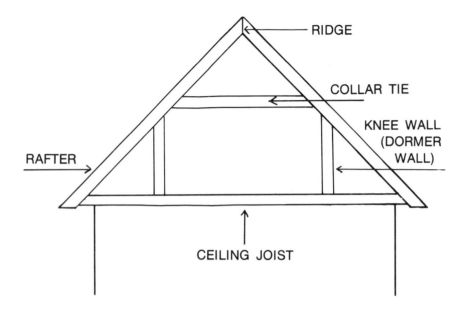

Fig. 23. Collar ties and knee walls strengthen a roof.

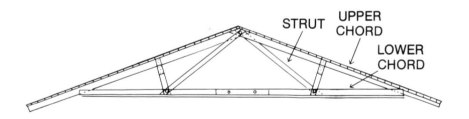

Fig. 24. The W type truss. Trusses aligned — one following the other — strengthen a roof. With truss construction a low pitched roof can withstand heavy snow load.

concrete), but a bituminous coating is recommended. Sometimes a plastic sheet placed snugly against the wall is satisfactory. Concrete- and cinder-block walls, on the other hand, because of the porous nature of the blocks, *must* be parged with the water-proofing concrete; the better builders will spray the bituminous material on in addition to the concrete.

Structural damage to the foundation walls, caused by undue settling of the house or by sinking of the footings holding these walls up, can cause serious cracks; however, you should not make a final judgment until the inside of the basement is inspected.

Wood foundation systems. Foundation walls are now being constructed of wood frame walls sheathed in plywood. Both the studs in the frame and the plywood are treated with a preservative to prevent decay and termite damage. Test houses are under observation that employ no concrete footing base; the foundation walls below the grade rest on a plank laid directly on gravel.

Slab-on-ground construction. In some areas of the country, especially in the south, houses are built over concrete slabs and do not have a basement. The slab serves as an underlayment for the finished floor. To provide support for the slab and the house above, footings are built underneath that slab. When the frost depth is less than a foot, the edge of this slab is thickened for support and serves as a footing. This type of construction is known as a monolithic slab/foundation construction.

It is important that the slab is poured over the proper foundation of gravel and vapor barrier (polyethylene sheeting) to prevent moisture migration into the concrete. In colder climates, it is also important that the slab has edge insulation, which prevents heat loss into the surrounding earth. This rigid or slab-type insulation should be placed vertically into the ground. It should be unicellular (foam plastic) to prevent moisture migration, and at least one inch thick. It usually extends into the ground about eighteen inches.

Resilient flooring such as asphalt tile can be placed over the slab, or can be covered with padding over which a rug is placed. Wall-to-wall carpeting and parquet floors can be used directly over the concrete.

The concrete slab sometimes includes radiant heating elements such as electric resistance elements or hot water pipes imbedded in the slab.

WALL STRUCTURES

Most walls fall into one of two basic categories: wood frame and masonry construction. There are advantages and disadvantages to both types. Climate and availability of materials play a large part in influencing the choice. In one area, house after house will be constructed of sandstone, while in another, glazed brick will be most common.

Wood frame construction

Sheathing. All exterior building materials should be applied over a sub-siding called *sheathing*. At one time, one by six inch boards with tar paper stapled on were nailed diagonally to the two by four inch studs, and these served as sheathing. Today, sheathing consists of pressed cellulose fiber in large four by eight foot sheets nailed to the studs. Sheathing material provides extra insulation to keep wind and water out, reducing sound transmission from outdoors, and even helps maintain structural rigidity.

Sheathing is usually black or tan, and its density grade is plainly visible, such as "Stronghold" or "Hi-density". Sheets with these designations will provide good bracing. Insulating quality is sometimes designated in large yellow letters; an "R" designation of 1.22 or 1.32 is not very significant in an insulated house but indicates a small contribution to heat flow resistance.

Unfortunately, in many newer houses where plywood is used for siding, sheathing is being eliminated. If possible, do not accept this when buying a house, even though it may be allowed by building codes. Without sheathing, the siding sometimes may not be waterproof, insulation from heat and noise is lost, wind penetrates, and rigidity is adversely affected.

There is also worry about the plywood because the sheets of glue between the laminated layers act as a vapor barrier near the outside of the house which is subject to cold temperatures. When a vapor barrier appears near a cold surface, condensation and harm to the wood-members can follow with time. The cellulose sheathing, on the other hand, doesn't offer this problem because it "breathes".

Siding. When a house is not covered on the side with masonry (brick, stone, etc.), the material covering the sheathing is known as siding. Clapboards, shingles, aluminum, and plywood are common types of siding. Stained or rough sawn plywood is popular today.

Siding made of pressed wood material, is in many cases better than wood; and does not expand or contract, crack, or split when you nail it. Most new houses at the time of writing make use of plywood, Masonite, or aluminum siding. These materials also serve as durable and attractive materials to cover the siding of older houses.

Aluminum siding comes from the factory in many shapes and sizes, including the most popular clapboard horizontal strips; of insulated and uninsulated, the former is slightly more expensive, but a better buy since it slightly reduces the cost of heating. Sometimes adding *insulated* aluminum siding is the only way to insulate the walls of an older house. It is also less apt to become permanently dented by baseballs or by rocks thrown from a lawnmower during grass cutting. Press the siding; if it gives, it is not insulated with fibrous or ridged backing.

Aluminum foil is a good reflective insulation if it is perforated to negate its tight vapor-barrier qualities. It can be placed under or next to aluminum siding, whether the siding is bare or thinly insulated. Condensation problems will occur, however, if used without the perforation in cold climates, resulting in woodframe damage.

A large number of builders and contractors in the United States are using the non-perforated, non-breathing type of aluminum foil—probably unwittingly—despite recommendations by the Architectural Aluminum Manufacturers' Association (AAMA). The AAMA Industry Standard 1403.1 of January 1971 states in part: "On underlayment apply aluminum *breather* foil with aluminum nails." Perforated aluminum foil should also be used directly behind other types of metal walls, such as steel.

Masonry Walls

The most common non-wood siding wall is masonry-stone, artificial stone, brick, or cement block. A good solid masonry house would have eight inches of masonry or brick, or four inches of concrete block covered by four inches of masonry facing.

Masonry walls are more expensive than wood frame walls. Masonry constructions, especially those made of brick and stone, have a prestige value that the houses with wood-siding walls do not. There are other advantages too: they do not sway as much in the wind as wood frame houses and usually do not develop plaster cracks as much as the frame houses; exterior maintenance is less; resistance to fire is better. Besides expense of construction, their greatest disadvantage is low insulation value. Old wood frame houses in cold climates — even without insulation — have offered more warmth. However, masonry will retain heat for long periods in winter and cold in summer because of its large mass and the nature of its composition.

The interior of the masonry wall should be furred with wood strips before plastering; this provides air space for insulation and prevents direct moisture contact. Older houses often are not furred on the inside walls and the condition is evidenced by moisture or efflorescence. Another method of waterproofing is to coat the interior face of the masonry with bituminous asphalt on tar, or to line it with a plastic membrane, before applying the finish to the wall.

Other Wall Types

Brick veneer. A combination of the frame and solid-masonry house is the brick veneer structure; this is a combination of brick facing and two by four framing. Essentially a frame house with four inches of brick, it offers a low-maintenance exterior. Because of the air space between the wood and wood-framing beneath it, it is also warm. The space between also offers a place to put duct work, electrical wires and plugs, and insulation. Sheathing should be secured next to the wood framing (e.g., between the framing and the brick).

To tell the difference between brick veneer and solid masonry, look for a header course every fifth or seventh course that appears in masonry brick walls. In brick veneer, there is no need for header courses because the brick veneer wall is secured by placing metal ties in the mortar joints and nailed to the studs.

Stucco. A stucco wall is one on which a coating of cement mortar is applied over sheathing or solid masonry in a manner similar to plaster. To provide good adherence to the sheathing, the coating is usually applied over metal lath. Stucco over cinderblock or structural clay tile is popular in warmer climates. Frequently applied coatings are covered with small pea-sized gravel. Many finish designs and attractive colors are possible with the use of this material.

Stucco over frame construction is more apt to have scattered cracking than stucco over masonry. Tapping the walls will usually reveal which type; the stucco on masonry sounds more solid.

THE WINDOWS

Types of Windows

One's choice of window in a house is largely a matter of design and architectural aesthetics, although climate has some influence. Windows are usually classified by the method in which they open and the material of which they are made (e.g., a "steel casement" window).

Double-hung windows. The most common window is the wooden double-hung window—so called because it consists of

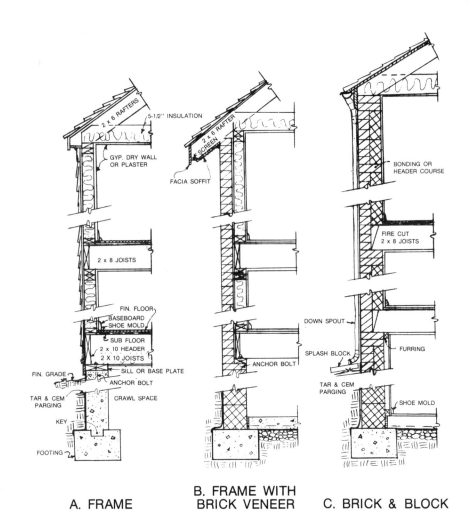

A. FRAME

B. FRAME WITH BRICK VENEER

C. BRICK & BLOCK

Fig. 25. Sectional views of three types of walls.

60

two parts, a lower sash and an upper sash, each working independently of the other. The typical design consists of six panes in each sash. If the upper and lower sashes each have six panes, the window would be called a six over six, or 6/6. Other types are 8/8. An early colonial design is a 12/6 window, the upper sash being larger. Some windows have single sheets of glass for each sash with a removable plastic arrangement that gives the appearance of six panes per sash.

The wooden double-hung window, if it is weather stripped, is a very warm window. It is also a tight window. More recently, aluminum double-hung windows have been used; they require little maintenance, but have more problems with insulation and condensation.

Many older double-hung windows, particularly in the upper sashes, are paint-bound and take considerable work to loosen. Try opening them when you make your indoor inspection.

Casement windows. Steel and aluminum casement windows, commonly used in old-English architecture, are attractive but, troublesome. Because of the high heat conductivity of the metal and the lack of effective lap or seal against the wind, the steel gets cold and condenses water out of the air in cold weather; thus heat loss and condensation are common problems. All casements except aluminum must be kept well-painted to avoid rust. The operating hardware of casements is usually a crank or lever arrangement, and should be checked during inspection for proper operation. A few wood casements are still around. If weather-stripped, they are warm and offer no condensation problems; however, they are expensive, and old ones rot on the upper vertical rail because of their exposure when swung out.

Sliders. Aluminum slider windows are low in maintenance because there is no need for counter-weights, hinges, or cranks. Many of these have pile runners and seal tighter than casement windows. They are low in cost, but subject to condensation problems.

Awning windows. Awning windows swing up and out like a big jalousie or the blade of a big venetian blind. They may be left open during a rainstorm to let the cool air in and to keep water

61

out. With their horizontal look, they are styled principally for contemporary and traditional houses, and not for the colonial style. Aluminum types are used extensively in southern climates.

Jalousie windows. Similar to awning windows in their operation, jalousie windows are usually made of aluminum. The outward and upward swinging panes lap eath other when closed, much as a venetian blind. The glass panes have no frame work. They are used as prime windows in southern climates, and for porch enclosure and remodelling in colder climates.

Insulating Windows

Double-glazed windows. Most of the windows described above can have vacuum sealed double panes (called insulated or double-glazed panes). The double panes are very effective and take the place of storm windows. They can, on occasion, develop a leak in the seal that holds air between the two panes, causing discoloration and insulation loss. Double vacuum glazed windows are often called Thermopane windows, a trade name.

Storm windows. Storm windows are a valuable bonus because they will save many dollars in heating and air conditioning costs; a ten per cent fuel saving is average for colonial style, the percentage rising for contemporary architecture with large window areas.

Today most storm windows are framed with aluminum. They are practical because they serve as combination windows with self-storing screens for mild weather. In colder climates of the country, windows of aluminum or wood should be provided with vent holes at the frame bottom to reduce condensation; condensation can occur when moist air from the house seeps through cracks into the air space. The holes in aluminum windows are often adjustable. Trial and error during cold weather, with careful monitoring of ice or fog on the inner side of the storm window, will help in making the adjustment. In wood windows, two 3/4 inch holes, drilled in the lower part of the frame, are usually satisfactory.

Two bonus features of aluminum storm windows are the extra security against burglars, and the reduced maintenance because the prime window does not often need painting.

Many older homes have home-made storm windows made of plastic sheeting. These, if they are not securely fastened by sand-wiching them between wood frames, will rip and tear even in a moderately high wind — but it is surprising how much punishment they will take if properly framed. Polyvinyl chloride sheeting (P.V.C.) will stand weathering much better than the polyethylene (P.E.) sheeting.

Plastic panes are becoming available for replacement purposes; they have a safety advantage, but are soft and scratch easily.

Window Security

For the sake of safety from burglary, it is better if the first floor windows are high off the ground. Consider all forms of security, starting with the safety locks on windows and doors as well as bars and grills. (See Chapter 8 for more information on locks and security.)

DOORS IN YOUR HOUSE

A front door should never be less than thirty-six inches wide; if it is, the house should always have another door that is at least this wide. Secondary exits such as a basement or a kitchen door should be thirty-two inches. Height should be either six feet eight inches or seven feet. An exterior door should be of solid construction, not of the hollow-core variety of two wood veneer panels with pieces of cardboard and wood framing sandwiched between; you can usually tell by tapping. Side and back doors can be made of glass sliding for viewing the yard, but the aesthetic value gained must be weighed against the heat loss introduced by the large glass area.

The front door telegraphs the personality of your house to a visitor. Both the present-day wooden doors and metal doors are beautiful, but the metal door may offer trouble when the house sinks through the years (as they all do); you can't shave it off at the edges like you can with a wood door.

Every door — front, back or side — should have a stepdown to the outside, a sill forming the bottom part of the frame and entrance. This eight-inch stepdown is for prevention of water coming in during heavy rains or snow.

Storm Doors

Storm doors for all entrances are a must in cold climates. They should be designed for easy changeover from screens in summer to glass inserts in winter. Good styling for the front storm door can add to the appearance of a house and, surprisingly, also to the resale value. A fancy storm door can cover up a nondescript front door. Good quality storm doors are available in aluminum or wood.

Weather stripping. Weather stripping is made of bronze, aluminum or plastic strips surrounding the door frames. These are more durable than the felt strips usually used in weatherproofing. Look for this weatherproofing and for openings or cracks between the door frame and the rest of the building. These cracks normally occur with sinking of the house, and if filled completely with caulking material will cause no trouble.

An interlocking or pressure-adjusting sill plate should be installed under the bottom edge of all weather-exposed doors to keep out the wind and rain.

Door security. For security against burglary, safety latches on doors are advisable. A lock that will open only with a key from both sides is recommended in high crime areas. With this type of lock the burglar, if he breaks the glass in the door, will be unable to open the door without a key. (See Chapter 8, which discusses locks and other security measures.)

PORCHES AND STOOPS

If porches and stoops are exposed, they collect water; if not on proper footings, they sink and pull away from the house. Thus cracks between the floors of these porches or stoops frequently appear even in new houses.

Do not prematurely judge a house by faulty stoops. Because the stoop is not attached to the main structure, the pull-away is not indicative of the condition of the main wall structure.

Wood porches should have good ventilation underneath to avoid rot. It is best to have a porch decking spaced so there is 1/4 to 1/8 inch between each board. Tongue and groove decking rots out quickly. Look carefully at the porch roof; often the roof is constructed with a shallow pitch to keep it below second story windows and, if of the shingle type, it may leak or show signs of wear more than other parts of the house.

INSECT INFESTATION

Termites. Termites are insects that thrive on wood or cellulose products. As is well known, they are particularly fond of wood in houses. Termites live in colonies like ants. They travel through tunnels the size of a straw to the earth every one or two days to obtain water. It is these mud tunnels on the surface or in the eaten wood that are an indication of past or present termite activity. The most likely place to find them is in porches, stoops and outdoor stairways, or any place that is damp, dark, and close to the ground. The best cure is to block these pathways, or to poison the soil.

Termites usually take their meals in the wood closest to the earth. A good place to look is underneath a porch where the wood is touching or near the ground. You can see evidence of the bugs at the ends of joists or on the wooden plate (two by eight) that the first floor rests on. Look also under basement stairs or on window sills close to the ground.

Termite shields of metal strips were extensively used in high-density termite localities. The shield is a physical barrier laid over the foundation at some point above ground before the wood framing above begins. It offers some discouragement to the erection of termite tunnels but does not do away with them as well as soil poisoning.

If you decide to buy a house that you suspect of having termites, or that has termites, call in professional help. If the company you contact is reputable, they will tell you if the house is free of infestation, and will issue a one-year warranty. If treatment is required they will use poison—a chemical—which can be effective for ten years or so, and even for fifteen to twenty years if the soil around the house is relatively dry. The technique the professionals use consists of injecting the chemical into the soil under pressure. Chlordane is the most widely-used and can be purchased by the homeowner.

The signs of recent termite treatment are small covered holes about the size of a quarter; you will find them in the ground about eighteen to twenty-four inches apart, and inside in the basement concrete floor next to a wall (and in the wall if it is hollow). These holes are drilled for the chemical poison injection.

The presence of termites usually carries a scare factor many times larger than the amount of damage caused. However, if left to colonize and prosper for a number of years, the damage can be extensive.

Always be certain that there is a complete understanding between you and the seller as to the extent of the damage before you close a deal. Never close a deal without a certificate prepared by a competent professional certifying absence of termites or termite treatment. The contract should state that "seller shall furnish a certificate that the house is free of visible action, infestation and visible damage." Make sure that the contract also states that "a warranty to include treatment shall be given the purchaser along with the certificate in the event termites do occur within a period of one year."

Other wood-boring insects. A house buyer will often be needlessly frightened by other insects that live around wood. For example, the carpenter bee, which is the size of a bumble bee,

Fig. 26a. The termite: straight body, no waist.

Fig. 26b. The flying ant: a pinched waist.

will drill a hole about the size of his body into wood porch structural members and spew sawdust on the ground. The boring is harmless if you get rid of him with a non-lethal dose of an insect spray.

Damaging insects are the powder post beetles, or "wood borers". They work slowly in dry wood, soften patches of it and leave a white powder behind. Professional help is recommended, but you can remove them yourself by applying any clear wood preservative whose active ingredients include pentachlorphenol, tetrachloraphenol and other chlorinated phenols. With a little sanding, cutting, filling with plastic wood and repainting, the damaged structures can be made to look almost like new.

The carpenter ants, which bore into damp wood and leave a tell-tale sawdust, can also cause damage. Professional help is recommended for their permanent removal. The damp, partially destroyed wood should be replaced if damage is structural. If decorative, putty and paint. The worker ants, or the females, are among the largest known ants, and are approximately 1/2 inch long. They enter the house by dropping from trees, and are attracted to leaky damp areas, such as under a flat-roof porch at the columns and beams.

4. LOOKING AT THE
INTERIOR CONSTRUCTION

THE BASEMENT

After making your outdoor examination, go down into the basement. Try to relate your examination to outside indicators, such as water from faulty gutters and downspouts. Look for cracks in the walls, indicating inverse grade sloping and sinking of foundation.

Leaky basement. A good indicator of past flooding—and a very unscientific one—is the way things are stored about the basement. If you see important papers, personal momentos or heirlooms lying on the floor, you can be almost certain that you are looking at a dry basement.

On the other hand, if you see rust stains, paint peel, mildew or efflorescence, you are probably looking at a damp basement, and maybe a basement that has previously and regularly been flooded. Look at the baseboard for rusty nails. Remove an electric plate to examine rust on the junction box. Look under the furnace; the previous owner may have painted the floor to cover tell-tale signs but forgot to paint this area. Rust around the furnace frame is also an indication of continual wetness.

Floor tiles with whitish markings at the joints indicate continued flooding. At the baseboard, blackened and soft wood rather than just one water ring, is a bad sign. Continued dampness may be accompanied by excessive joist sag and squeaky floor above. Numerous cracks in the concrete floor can be caused by water pressure beneath. The deeper the basement is in the ground, the greater is the water pressure against the wall — a situation which could bring water into the basement. (For some hints on waterproofing a basement see Chapter 10.)

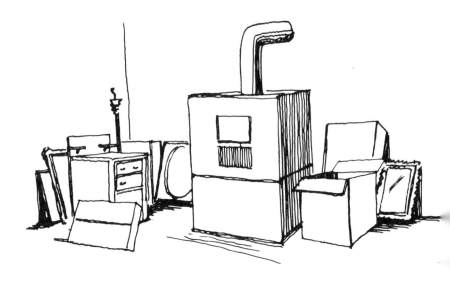

Fig. 27. Rubbish, old pictures and heirlooms in the basement indicate that there has been no continual trouble with leaks.

Analyzing cracks in basements. It is more difficult to evaluate the significance of cracks in new than in old houses, where there is a measuring stick of time. In the older house, the house has probably settled and cracking has been arrested. If a house is forty years old and has a crack of about one inch in thickness (which has probably been patched), one might safely say to himself, "Well, that is 1/40 of an inch a year. Is that significant, really?"

See how many times the crack has been patched and reopened by movement of the house. Different shades of mortar or patching material will tell you this. If you know when the walls were painted, see if there is paint in the crack. If there is not, the crack occurred after painting and indicates that there probably will be more problems with cracks in the future.

Basement floor cracks with sag sloping to the outer walls is a further indication of movement. A bend in the joists which slopes to the outside walls is an indication of undue foundation settlement. When this occurs, the floor above will also slope to the outside.

Horizontal cracks in basements of older houses do not constitute the danger that stepped and vertical cracks do, particularly if the stepped crack widens as it extends upward. If the grade is low around the house, you are apt to see a horizontal line-crack on the inside wall along the frost-line zone. Yards that are not drained properly will cause this. The dirt becomes saturated around the wall creating lateral thrust by the hydrostatic push of the wet soil. Swelling of the earth takes place because of freezing and thawing, also exerting push. These cracks are not visible on the outside, where there is a pinching effect with the opening on the inside.

This lateral thrust can be relieved by filling dirt around the walls, so the grade slopes away from the house and carries off downspout discharge. High and dry earth built up around the house may also help to stabilize the sinking of a stoop which is beginning to pull away from the house.

New houses often have a long horizontal crack and bulge inside the basement wall. This is due to lateral pressures exerted during backfill operations, and aggrevated by wet, heavy, and loose clay saturated during construction. (The lateral pressures during this period exceed the vertical pressures.) This bulging and cracking may be serious, and will be difficult to analyze. It is an indication of wall weakness, so it deserves weighty attention. You should consult a home inspection service and ask the builder for a long-time guarantee of wall soundness — you might choose to buy elsewhere. It should be comforting to know,

71

however, that the soil condition will improve each year with normal weather and temperature.

Vertical or stepped cracks in a corner which widen at the top can indicate that a footing is sinking at the corner. If of real importance, the crack will go all the way through the wall and extend upward the entire height of the building. Severe footing failure is more easily discernible in a house of all masonry construction because of the rigidity of the house. These cracks, of course, will not appear in a frame house on the outside, but you can look on the inside walls and plaster near the roof for indications of sinking foundations.

It should now be apparent to the reader that evaluations of cracking must include inspection of the outside, basement, floors and upper inside walls, and that the measuring stick of time must be considered along with information gained from adjacent houses.

Wet basements. Water and damp walls in a house under construction has worried many prospective buyers. However, it would be unusual for any house not-graded or where gutters are not yet installed, to be dry. Nevertheless, note this condition on your checkout list to the builder.

Wood framing. Examine the wood framing above you and check for bowing and sagging of joists, spanning of joists, sizes and spacing between them. A sag in the basement joists means a sag in the floor above. If a house is spanned with 2 x 8's, sixteen inches apart, and the span is twelve feet or less, the floor above will be firm. A span over twelve feet may produce excessive bounce. Joists, two by ten inches in size, will carry up to fourteen feet rigidly, with bounce developing over fourteen feet. They should not have a span length of more that sixteen feet. Bridging between a span with x-bracing or solid wood blocks between joists, will stiffen the floor and firm up larger span lengths than outlined above. Joists doubled up in parallel under a partition above is a good indication of a well-framed house. Conversely, undersized joists and excessive span-lengths indicate that studs and rafters in the upper part of the house are undersized, and that the contractor has taken short cuts in construction.

At some places in the basement a beam of wood or steel will support bearing partitions and joists above. This beam will more than likely have its ends resting on the outside walls and be supported in the middle by columns of brick, steel, or, as seen in very old homes, a column of wood. Wood beams sag with age, particularly if overspanned or exposed to excessive dampness in the basement. Steel and brick have the advantage of being fire resistant in addition to deterring termites and rot.

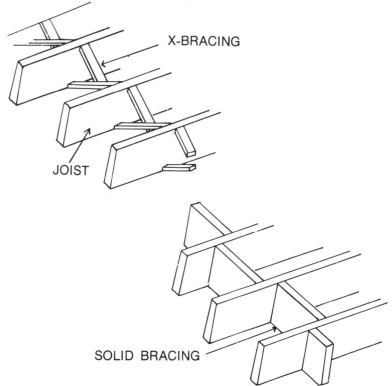

X-BRACING

JOIST

SOLID BRACING

Fig. 28. X-bracing and solid bracing will stiffen the floor above.

Courtesy of National Forest Products Association.

Basement insulation. In these days of energy shortages it is best that insulation be placed between the joists of ceilings in little-used and cool basements, to minimize heat loss from upstairs. Two inch, R-7, glass fiber blanket material is ample. If reflective insulation is attached to the glass fiber blanket, the shiny material should be towards the warm floor above. Leave an air-space. The flanges on the side of the blanket should be nailed securely to the joists. Basements receiving much use should have furred walls with insulation behind. (Directions for constructing these furred walls with insulation are given in Chapter 10.)

Habitable requirements for basements. A basement should have at least seven feet six inches of head room, and eight feet or more if the ceiling is loaded with ducts and pipes. Adequate lighting and ventilation is necessary. Fire exits are a must. If there is not more than one door, windows that offer easy exit are needed. The furnace room should be closed off and still fit into a good floor plan. A floor drain in the utility section will prevent damage to the finished area in the event of accidental water overflow. In some code jurisdictions the basement must have area at the ground level before it can be legally habitable for living and sleeping use.

CRAWL SPACES

Houses without basements or concrete slab bases have a space underneath the ground floor known as a crawl space. This space should be high enough to allow access to all corners. The recommended minimum is two feet clearance and preferably two and one-half feet. Most of these spaces are over dirt which gives off undesirable moisture. To eliminate this problem, a permanent plastic sheeting with heavy overlap between the sheets should be laid over the dirt in order to serve as a moisture seal.

Insulation in crawl space. One way to insulate this space is to place fiberglass blanketing between the floor joists. A total thickness of about four inches (R13) is recommended. The vapor barrier or reflective insulation should be placed on the warm side of the fibrous insulation and towards the floor. This prevents the barrier or aluminum surface from becoming cold and from collecting condensed water during cold weather. Such moisture can seriously impair the effectiveness of insulation. The flanges on the two sides of the blanketing should be nailed securely to the joist. Chicken wire should be placed below the loose blanket of fiberglass to hold it up. Any cross-supports for insulation that are widely spaced are ineffective.

When this method of insulation is used, it is important that there be adequate ventilation into a crawl space to blow away any moisture that may migrate into it. A minimum of one sq. ft. of cross-ventilation to each 1,500 square feet of crawl space is required if a moisture seal is provided. A window or lattice work around the perimeter of the space are common ways to provide the ventilation. It is also important that all pipes and ducts are well insulated.

The ducts, if used for air-conditioning and heating, must have a vapor barrier around the outside of the insulation to keep the hot, humid summer air away from the cold metal to prevent condensation. During winter, this vapor barrier will not cause trouble because the heat from the ductwork will keep the insulation temperature above the dewpoint temperature (See glossary)—the point in temperature where condensation occurs. R-7 glass fiber duct-wrap, about two inches thick; and foil backed, will suffice except in exceptionally cold climates. The foil should be placed on the outside.

Water pipes require two inches of R-7 glass fiber insulation. If these pipes carry cold spring water, the insulation should have a vapor barrier.

In some houses, crawl spaces are insulated with perimeter insulation. This means the insulation is placed around the inside of the four walls instead of between the floor joists. The method is advantageous because it is not necessary to insulate the pipes and ducts below the floor. However, this type of insulation is useless if there are ventilation louvers to let in cold ventilating air, and inadequate if moisture collects in the space either from the living quarters above or from the ground. All the more reason that the ground must be covered with a vapor barrier of plastic sheeting!

In houses which rest only on piers and where there is no protective covering around the perimeter of the space, insulation under the floor and around the ductwork and pipes is especially important.

THE ATTIC

The following seven principal items for inspection should be observed when you look around in the attic:

- Insulation
- Ventilation
- Framing structure
- Signs of leaks, particularly at protrusions through the roof; i.e., vents, etc.
- Fan exhausts, ducts, wires, and chimney
- Accessibility for storage space or future living quarters
- Firewalls between town-houses or other attached housing units

The insulation

Six inches of attic insulation is recommended by most authorities. In an unfinished attic, the insulation will usually be lying on the ceiling of the room below between the joists. It will be hidden below the attic flooring in a finished attic and a board should be pried up to examine it. The other alternative is to look back under the eaves, if they are accessible.

If the six-inch insulation is fiberglass or other types of blanket mineral wool, and was installed subsequent to 1969, it will have the designation R-19 printed on the attached Kraft paper vapor barrier. If it is about six and one-half inches thick it will have the designation R-22. It may have reflective insulation attached to one side. If so, the shiny metallic reflective insulation should be placed on the downward side next to the ceiling.

An excellent pamphlet giving information on insulation is published by the National Mineral Wool Insulation Association, 211 East 51 St., New York, N.Y., 10022. It is titled *How To In-*

Insulation addition. The addition of extra insulation is dependent upon the original insulation. When the original insulation is without reflective insulation, you have two choices. If the house has only two or three inches of glass fiber insulation between the joists *without* the shiny reflective insulation attached, you may bring the thickness up to six inches or even to a seven inch level — by "pouring" some loose mineral wool insulation over the initial blankets. (Loose mineral wool comes in bags, and it is necessary to scoop it out; the term "pour" is actually a misnomer used throughout the industry.) This is not advisable if there is an attic fan which could blow the loose material around, and it should not be placed near the ventilating louvers.

An alternative would be to add extra fiberglass blanket insulation. To do this, however, you should first remove the original blankets (without the reflective surface), and replace them with three or three and five-eighth inch blankets (R-11 or R-13) *with* reflective insulation attached; then put the original blankets back on top. Be sure that the reflective insulation faces downward and is next to the warm ceiling.

When the original insulation has reflective insulation attached, if it is two or three-inch stuff leave it where it is and add some bare three or three and five-eighth blankets (R-11 or R-13) minus the vapor barrier or the reflective aluminum sheet. A paper vapor barrier or aluminum sheeting sandwiched between two fiberglass layers may lead to condensation. Bare fiberglass blankets may not be easy to buy but you can get around this by buying blankets with only the vapor barrier, which you can then tear off. The bare insulation is not critical in a well ventilated attic.

For attic insulation, many contractors use insulation with Kraft paper for the vapor barrier instead of the metallic reflective insulation. This vapor barrier is slightly cheaper and almost as effective as the metallic sheeting. The shiny material is a better vapor barrier, but when it touches the drywall below it loses some of its radiation capability. It should be contiguous only with air.

When original insulation is loose mineral wool but increased thickness is needed, pour some more in. In old houses, the wool is thin, since it settles with time. This is one reason to make your final thickness more than six inches. Often the old insulation thickness varies markedly and should be leveled and filled.

Insulation between rafters. Some houses have blankets of fiberglass immediately below the roof and between the roof rafters; this method is not entirely satisfactory. If the house was built some years ago and has no ventilating louvers, moisture will migrate from below and cause condensation on very cold days (10° and below). Condensation occurs on the metal protuberances in the roof, such as nails and stack vents, thereby impairing the resistance of these blankets.

If the attic has vents, it will be cold and the extra insulation on the ceiling in winter will be almost useless. In the summer months, such insulation will help to insulate the attic air from the hot roof, but the money spent for this insulation would have been better spent in installing an attic fan to cut air conditioning costs. A fan can be helpful in winter months too, to dispel moist air which may cause trouble in near-zero weather. If the insulation between the roof-rafters is already there, leave it in because it will definitely help in the summer, and perhaps during the winter, providing there are no air vents.

Insulation of ductwork. It is mandatory that all metal duct work in the attic be covered with a vapor barrier if the ducts are for air conditioning and be insulated with at least one inch of fiberglass, preferably two inches (R-7). The vapor barrier should be on the outside of the insulation to keep moist summer air away from insulation. This arrangement is satisfactory for the ducts in winter when warm air is passing through them. (See discussion about insulating ducts and pipes in crawl spaces in this chapter.) Some metal ducts come with the insulation inside, which serves the same purpose.

Exposed, rigid, foamed-plastic insulation is not advisable in the attic because of the danger of fire and toxic fumes. The rigid material should never be kept exposed anywhere in the house, even though it is usually treated with a fire retardant material.

Ventilation in the attic

Ventilation of the attic space is important, particularly because of the need to keep the insulation dry. When moist air from the living quarters below seeps up into the attic on a cold day, condensation may occur; this can lessen the effect of the insulation and on a long-term basis even cause damage to the ceiling below. To provide this ventilation, nearly all homes built in the last twenty-five years have louvers somewhere in the attic — at the ends, underneath the soffits, or at the ridge. Usually only two relatively large ones are provided when they are at the ends, a number of smaller ones when they are underneath the soffits, and just one when at the ridge. The one at the ridge is covered, of course, to protect it from rain and snow. End louvers or a ridge louver in combination with soffit vents make a good combination, because a natural thermal current develops. The important thing is that the total area of the louvers is sufficient to provide the necessary air movement. Louvers should be screened to prevent entry of birds into the attic.

An aggregate *free* area of one square foot for each three hundred square feet of attic floor area is often recommended. A better procedure for obtaining sufficient ventilation is to allow one square inch of *overall* vent area for each square foot of floor area. More area may be needed in southern states and less area in northern states. For end vents, the area should not be too much greater in colder climates; heavy winds may blow snow on the attic floor.

The attic without ventilation frequently presents condensation problems in the winter. When the temperature is 10° or below, metal, in the form of nails, stackvent and other roof protuberances, quickly becomes cold and condensation will cause water to drip down; this causes damage to structural members below.

Sometimes when the water starts to drip from the metal parts, whether or not there is insulation, homeowners will open a door to the attic to allow warm air to rise from downstairs. The warm air is full of moisture and only worsens the condition. A better way is to open two attic windows, if there are any.

Ventilation is just as important in the summer. Attic spaces, even with ventilation, can reach 140 degrees, thus warming the ceiling below and placing a big load on the air-conditioning system. You can test the attic of a house on a hot day with a thermometer in the attic and one in the shade outside. If there is more than a fifteen or a twenty degree difference, more ventilation is required. It is an established fact that a cooler attic will save on air-conditioning. Ventilation can be increased with an attic fan to blow air through the louvers; this will save even more on air-conditioning costs. (See Chapter 7 for more details on attic fans.)

Roof framing

The roof framing will vary with each house. In the conventional rafter type used in older houses, the framing members should be sixteen inches apart, center to center of the member (sixteen inch O.C.). Mimimum size for a rafter or ceiling joist should be two by six inches. Long spans in areas of heavy snow loads should be two by eight inches in size. Additional bracing, such as knee-walls and/or collar beams, strengthen long spans and keep the house more rigid.

If you fail to see knee-walls or collar beams in the attic, you may see plaster or dry-wall cracks in the upstairs rooms at the corners; these are caused by outward thrust of the rafters. A crack may also develop directly beneath a knee-wall, which is in direct contact with the roof; since it is exposed to extreme temperatures, it may set up a weight-transfer or moving between members. If a new roof covering of shingles is being planned for the house, the extra weight may make collars and/or knee-walls a necessity.

The truss roof is often used in the attics of new houses. Truss members are made up of 2 x 4's and 2 x 3's or 2 x 4's for short struts. The rafter, or top chord, and the bottom chord, which is actually the attic floor, are trussed together with triangular braces that transfer the weight of the roof to the outside walls of the house. The use of trusses eliminates the need for load-bearing partitions below the attic and roof. It is cheaper to install, but eliminates much of the storage space. (See Fig. 24)

Pipes, ducts, wires, and chimney

Electrical or plumbing blunders appear frequently in new houses and can be left over and potentially dangerous in old houses. Watch out for wire splices that are not correctly placed in metal junction boxes. If there is a bathroom below the attic without windows and depending on an exhaust fan, make sure that the fan-duct comes up and goes through the roof or to one of the end attic louvers.

If a kitchen fan-duct comes up into the attic, it should be ducted to the outside; otherwise, it could be a fire hazard as well as a source of undesirable moisture. This is often missed in new houses simply because builders do not always check their houses thoroughly.

Examine all items that protrude through the roof, including the stack vents that release gases from the sewer system. Make sure you cannot see daylight above where the protuberance passes through the roof. If you do, it means a flashing repair job on the roof is necessary.

Often air-conditioning equipment will be placed in the attic. There can be serious oversights and blunders made during the installation of this equipment. (Detailed information on what to look for is discussed in Chapter 6.)

Signs of leaks

On cold days inspect nails and other metal protuberances in the roof for moisture. Look for water stain marks on the roof boards (roof deck) and correlate these with ceiling stains and the

81

plaster of the rooms beneath.

In tracing leaks remember that the leak stains showing below are usually not directly under the leak. The water, held by surface tension, will run down a rafter until it comes in contact with a vertical framing member and then will drip and run straight down. When it hits the plaster ceiling it may show a stain but will run back to the lowest part of the ceiling in the middle of the room, where sag is usually greatest. Often if water is in quantity, it will come through the ceiling light.

Attic use

An attic with a floor and plenty of room to walk around in is an asset for any house. It would provide good storage space and a place to bring your children or grandchildren to show your old clothes and heirlooms. It may even be made into a room for one of the teenagers when a new crop of children makes the house crowded. Small access doors are easily converted to pull-down stairways, and upstairs hall arrangements allow for permanent stairs if there is none already.

The fire-wall

If you are in the attic of a town-house or an attached house, look for masonry firewalls between your attic and adjacent ones. A firewall is absolutely essential and is required by most building codes, yet is left out in many complexes. In December, 1972, in Greenbelt, Maryland, fire swept through seventeen town-houses, spreading through an open attic that was common to all. Twelve houses were gutted completely. A similar instance happened in Columbia, Maryland, prompting a code change.

5. THE FINISHED INTERIOR

This part of the inspection will be done more rapidly, as there are fewer basic structural components to judge.

THE FLOORS

Wood-strip flooring. The oldest and probably most popular flooring is the wood strip type. Most houses built before 1965 have hard-oak floors which, if kept up, add to the beauty of a home as well as to the resale value. However, if they are dirty and marked-up, cleaning by re-sanding can be expensive. They can also be squeaky and buckled.

Sometimes houses over forty years old will have oak floors downstairs and softwood pine or fir upstairs. Strip flooring such as oak or pine tends to make the floors rigid and to deaden sound transmission. A well-built house will always have the flooring nailed over a subfloor.

Squeaky floors do not necessarily indicate a problem. All wood-strip floors tend to squeak somewhere and they can sometimes be cured of this be renailing at the framing joists or screwing the boards down. Wedging from below, if access is possible, will also help. You can also try talcum powder between the cracks; this acts as a filler and lubricant.

Parquet floors. Parquet floors are made of short hardwood strips prefabricated into nine by nine or twelve by twelve inch squares. The squares are later placed into position onto the floor, and can be quite attractive. Since they tend to loosen up with the years, push down on a few of them when inspecting an old house.

Parquet floors require a smooth subfloor, made of 1/2 inch or 5/8 inch plywood, or smooth composition underlayment if over rough one by six subflooring. Parquet blocks may also be applied directly to concrete floors with mastic.

Resilient floors. Resilient floors include composition floors, asphalt tile, vinyl tile and sheet goods such as linoleum; they are used in many parts of the house, particularly in bathrooms, kitchens and recreation rooms. Of these, vinyl tile has the best sheen, lasts longest, and offers the most attractive designs. Commercial examples are *Excellon, Pacemaker,* and *Solarium.* Some are used on the first floors of basementless houses over the slab at grade level. Asphalt tile is the cheapest and, although less dense, may be the best buy for an economy budget.

Any resilient floors that are installed over wood framing must be installed over a subfloor 5/8 inch thick, tongue and groove, well-sanded and made of plywood. If it is either thinner than this or rough, a smooth underlayment of thinner composition board will be needed over the subfloor. Proper fastening of this underlayment to the framing is important to prevent squeaking. Screw nails or coated nails should be used. Most manufacturers of the resilient material recommend that it be nailed every twelve inches. Because joists are usually placed sixteen inches apart, this means it becomes necessary to nail every eight inches if every other nail is to go through the underlayment and into a joist. Blocking with 2 x 4's perpendicular to the joists helps prevent the edge joints from giving under weight.

Resilient floors that are installed over concrete slab should be placed only on a well-drained dry slab. When below-grade slabs, as in a basement, are to be covered, certain rough tiles and linoleum are not recommended. Asphalt tile applied with an asphalt emulsion has good adherence if dampness occurs and is probably the safest to use.

When any floor is exposed to the weather, such as floors under protruding sections of a house, it should be insulated at least two and one-quarter inch with R-11 blanket material.

Carpeting. Since the '60's, project builders often used carpeting instead of flooring because of its glamour and low cost. Carpeting usually is placed over a subfloor made of plywood. Unless a very good carpet is used, a homeowner will be confronted within three to five years with worn out carpeting, necessitating a major expense.

And it is important that this subflooring be at least 5/8 inch thick and preferably made of tongue and groove stock. Builders will often skimp on this. In a new house try to check on this before the carpet is laid, or check for thickness from the basement, where pipes and ducts go through the first floor.

A new technique for securing the plywood to the joists employs the use of mastic spread on the top of joist edges. The plywood is then glued and sparsely nailed.

When checking a new house walk heavily over all carpeted areas and listen to how well the plywood is attached. A clapping or rumbling sound indicates failure of the glue/nail attachment. It is, unfortunately, very common.

Carpeting today is made principally of either wool or synthetic fibers (commonly known as plastic). Of these fibers, *Acrylic, Nylon, Polyester,* and *Olefin* (Polypropylene) are the most common. Wool carpeting is the old standby and, if of good construction, the homebuyer has certainty of durability and longevity. However, even the best wools have disadvantages not found in synthetic fiber carpeting: they are subject to damage of moths, unless treated at the factory; they can be weakened by salt, ammonia, alkaline soaps, chlorine bleaches, and strong detergents; they can be damaged by mildew. Wool manufacturers claim that resistance to fire is good and, when compared to some synthetic fibers, they probably have a case.

Synthetic fibers also offer many advantages. They can be tougher than wool, easier to clean, more resistant to acids and solvents, and less apt to fuzz as much as wool. Of course, this is not applicable to all synthetic fiber carpeting. The prospective buyer must compromise, using the following guide of synthetic fiber carpeting before passing final judgment on the carpeting in the house being inspected.

Over wood floor or plywood subfloor, the carpet is usually laid without nails or adhesive; it is tightened underneath at the edges with flat wood strips with nails protruding upward from underneath.

Carpeting can be glued directly to a concrete floor. The adhesive used must be matched to the carpet backing, and nearly 100 percent of the backing should have contact with the adhesive. The concrete must be absolutely dry before gluing takes place. This is important for a concrete slab in a slab-on-grade house, and is one reason why vapor barrier sheeting must be placed underneath the slab.

ACRYLICS: Resemble wool in appearance. Resist aging well. Have good resilience, abrasive resistance and resistance to soiling. Good resistance to mildew. Are superior to wool in resistance to most acids and solvents. Fair to good resistance to weak, cold alkalis. Only disadvantages are pilling and fuzzing, and retention of oily stains. Some acrylics burn readily; others pass flame spread requirements. Generally acrylics have good resistance to sunlight.

MODACRYLICS: Are a modified acrylic fiber and have reduced flammability. Resistance to abrasion only fair. Good colorfastness and resistance to chemicals, moths and mildew. Unaffected by alkalis. Some loss in tensile strength may be noted by certain brands upon prolonged exposure to sunlight.

NYLON: Have very good abrasive resistance, resilience and flame resistance. They absorb water so slowly that water stains are easily removed. Unaffected by weak acids and solvents, but will decompose in strong mineral acids. Nylon carpeting in particular needs a good backing for dimensional stability. Disadvantages are about the same as for acrylics in that they tend to pill and fuzz, and to retain oily stains. Some discoloration may result from prolonged exposure to sunlight. Nylon has more sheen than wool and some of the other synthetics.

POLYESTERS: Have a soft and luxurious appearance, good wear resistance, and colorfastness. The resilience of polyester is somewhat less than that of nylon and some other types so that dense, deeper pile construction is needed for the same performance. Excellent resistance to mildew. Flame resistance good. Have good dimensional stability. However, they will pill, and stain with oily materials. In some instances, prolonged exposure to sunlight will result in some loss of strength.

OLEFINS: Excellent resistance to most acids and alkalis. Not attacked by mildew. Good resistance to aging, abrasion, and indirect sunlight. Can be treated at the factory to give good resistance to direct sunlight. Used for indoor-outdoor carpets.

RAYONS: Unaffected by most acids and solvents. With low pile and with dense and not fuzzy construction, is flame resistant. Not resilient to oily stains. Has only fair-to-poor resistance to abrasive wear. Soils rapidly. Avoid any fuzzy type of rayon carpeting or rug because of fire danger.

Surface flammability. A fiber that will burn readily in its natural state can be made into a carpet that complies with Government flammability standards. For the consumers' protection, the Flammable Fabrics Act requires that all large carpets and carpet tiles manufactured or imported after April 16, 1971, must comply with Department of Commerce Standard FF 1-70.

Standard FF 1-70 was established to protect you against unreasonable risk of carpet fires from small ignition sources such as fireplace embers, lighted cigarettes and matches. However, it does not insure a carpet's complete fire resistance.

Surface textures. Two popular types of surface texture for wool and synthetic carpeting are the *sculptured* and *plush* (cup-pile) types. The sculptured type is composed of designs created by alternating areas with and without the heavy pile. The plush type, common in large halls and lobbies of theaters, has a constant pile thickness; it is more likely to show footmarks than the sculptured type.

Another texture is *level loop pile*, which wears well and hides footprints. The *frieze* or twist type wears well and hides footprints, dirt and dust; if it has a level surface is not difficult to clean.

Over ninety-five percent of all carpet made in the United States is tufted. Tufting is done by hundreds of yarn threaded needles operating at high speed. As the needles are pushed through a backing fabric, loops, or tufts are formed and held in place by a primary backing. Only three percent of all carpets made in the United States is woven.

One tufted type, shag carpeting, has reached an increasing popularity in the 1970's. Shags come in a wide range of colors and textures, lend a casual look, and are both durable and moderately priced. They're available with medium pile lengths to the elegant four-to-six inch lengths. They come in two-tone styles, and are sometimes printed.

Some people don't like shag carpeting with long pile length because it requires vacuum cleaners with a special suction feature. Sometimes, when the pile is heavy, it requires raking with a special small rake about twice a week.

Shag carpeting with long pile length should be avoided on steps because of the difficulty of vacuuming or raking. The heavy pile may also cause someone to trip and fall. Carpeting with long pile length is probably safe, however, for children who love to play on steps; the heavy pile will cushion their falls, which will occur regardless of carpeting material.

Indoor-outdoor carpeting. Indoor-outdoor carpeting is used in many homes today. It is safer than in 1968, when there was evidence and great concern that it could catch fire easily. Tests made in 1973 by Consumers' Union indicate that the danger has nearly disappeared.

The two main types of indoor-outdoor carpeting are needle-punched and needle-tufted. Needle-punched carpets are thinner and lighter than needle-tufted, and look like felt or padding. The needle-tufted models more closely resemble conventional carpets; they are mainly used in recreation rooms, basements or front porches or stoops. For more detailed information on indoor-outdoor carpets, see the August 1973 issue of *Consumer Reports*.

How to check carpeting

1. Examine pile density. Pile density is one of the best indications of quality. Brush your hand over the surface of the carpet to feel if the pile is thick, tight and springy. Fold a corner of the carpet (if not yet fastened down); if much backing shows through the pile, the density is low. (This test may not be valid for a shag carpet.)

2. Examine method of installation of wall-to-wall carpeting. Edges to accommodate irregularities or obstructions in the wall-trim should be neatly cut and trimmed; those at doorways should be protected by metal strips. Seams should be kept at a minimum, well hidden, and preferably out of traffic pattern; they should cause no unevenness in the grain or color. There should be no kinks, bumps, or wrinkles. Usually all carpeting should be installed in the same direction. Be sure you check to see that the doors clear the carpet easily when they are opened.

3. On cold, dry days test for static charge. Walk on the carpet and then touch a radiator or wall thermostat. If there is a spark, you'll have problems — which you can cure with a good humidifier.

Backing. Backing is the material that forms the back of the carpet, regardless of the type of construction. For example, the backing in a tufted carpet is the material to which surface yarns are attached. Sometimes a secondary backing is laminated to the primary backing, and acts as a padding. Both types of backing can be made of jute, KRAFT-CORD, cotton, woven or non-woven synthetic material. A common synthetic is olefin. If the secondary backing acts as a padding it will be made of a high density foam-like material.

The primary and secondary backings, not the type of fiber used for the pile yarn, determine the stability of the carpet. In general, jute backings provide greater stability than the common olefin backings.

Padding. Many carpets are made with high density sponge or latex foam rubber padding permanently attached. It should be at least 1/8 inch thick. Separate padding is used under most wall-to-wall and room-fit carpeting. Common types are felted, latex foam, or sponge rubber, and urethane foam.

Some padding is certified on the label as meeting FHA standards for cushioning under wall-to-wall carpeting; here you have assurance of quality. Other high-quality padding, however, has never been tested against the FHA standard.

A good booklet giving more detailed information on carpeting and padding is *Carpets and Rugs,* CIS-12, obtainable from the U.S. Government Printing Office, Washington, D.C. 20402.

The Carpet and Rug Institute of Dalton, Georgia, 30720, publishes a small booklet entitled *Carpets and Rugs, the Now Way to Choose Them;* it is free.

For those who specify, purchase, or sell commercial carpeting, the Carpet and Rug Institute publishes *The Carpet Specifier's Handbook.* This book is technical in nature and should not be requested from the Institute unless important technical questions need resolving.

WALLS AND CEILINGS

The Drywall. A drywall is comprised of large prefabricated panels of gypsum plaster sheathed in paper. When properly applied, it is similar to "wet plaster", which was used almost universally thirty years ago. There are advantages and disadvantages to both types. Probably the only significant advantage of wet plaster is that the finished thickness is 3/4 inches, whereas the normal drywall panels are 1/2 inch thick, not offering as much sound transmission resistance.

A good drywall installation will have its panels secured to the stud by a mastic material and with special nails designed to increase holding power. These nails include ring nails, screw nails, and rosin-coated box nails. Some builders will eliminate mastic application and use more nails.

A smooth continuity between panels is obtained by filling and trowelling the joints with a joint compound over a paper tape. The nail depressions are filled and trowelled. Then final finishing is accomplished by sanding and by "point-up" work. There should be no evidence of the panel joints once the walls are painted.

Drywall plaster is sold in several thicknesses. Remodellers often use 3/8 inch or even thinner to cover old walls; one-half inch is generally accepted as standard for new construction. Occasionally in expensive custom homes builders may use 5/8 inch or two layers of 3/8 inch. All sheets are sold in four foot widths and varying lengths; the twelve foot length is most popular in new construction. The larger sheets are installed horizontally and mean fewer joints.

If you see "nail-popping" in an old house (See Glossary), don't be discouraged. It's not alarming and can be fixed more easily than the characteristic wet plaster cracks that radiate outward from wall openings. The repair job can be done by removing the old nails and replacing them with the special dry-wall nails, or just add one of these special nails close to where each of the old ones was. Hammer the new nails in so the hammer-head makes a dimple into the board without breaking the paper. Finally, cover all nail heads or spaces with spackling compound, then trowel and sand.

Special finishes may be applied to drywall walls or ceilings, for example by applying a skim coat of "topping" compound. The skim coat may be left smooth, swished or dappled to obtain different texture.

Plaster. If you are considering a house built prior to the 1940's, chances are wet plaster is on the walls and ceilings. This has the advantage of better sound insulation, but little else. If, on a rare occasion, wet plaster is used in a new house, expect a good deal of moisture for a few months until it has fully dried. Also be prepared for openings in joints which will require filling.

Some cracks will occur in both dry and wet plaster, depending on the position of the walls in the house and the amount of settlement due to drying out and gravity. These cracks are usually not serious. (See Chapter 3 on foundations.) Expect to see a crack or two near a stairway. A partition with a door opening near an outside wall will often develop a harmless crack near the top of the jamb on the interior side of the partition.

Cracks are often apparent in ceilings below a bathroom, because of sudden changes in temperature and humidity and holes cut into joists to accommodate pipes. These will probably not increase with size and can be permanently repaired. Frame houses usually develop more cracks than brick or stone houses.

Water stains. Most five or six year old houses develop water stains on the ceilings under bathrooms from tub and shower spillage. In rare cases this is an indication of more serious problems, which are discussed in the plumbing section of Chapter 6. When examining the walls and ceilings throughout the upstairs, look for old water stains from possible roof leaks.

Special ceilings and walls. Ceiling tiles composed of such materials as composition board, plaster squares and metal are also used. Acoustical and fire-retardant materials come in many patterns and may be attached by gluing, nailing or hanging in metal grids; grid systems are known as suspended ceilings.

Attractive stucco ceilings and walls are found in many newer houses. These consist of a rough texture made by roughing the surface of a skim coat before it dries. Varied effects are obtained by daubing with a sponge, wadded newspaper or by swirling with an old, dry paintbrush; unfortunately, these attractive ceilings can be difficult to clean or make matching repairs.

Wood panelling. Wood and simulated-wood panelling is being used more and more these days for walls, principally because of variety and beauty, and also because it can be installed with less skill than either wet or dry plaster.

Plywood is very good for wood panelling on walls; it is durable and often adds richness to a family, recreation, or dining room. Wood facings such as elm, pecan, birch, and certain types of walnut are amenable to use on the plywood veneer. If these facings are used in their own thickness, they will twist, warp and split; by laminating them to a stable and less attractive wood, the result is excellent.

One problem is overall thickness on the walls. Some builders use 1/8 inch panelling, which is much too thin to stand rigidly between the framing members; it is actually meant for gluing over an existing wall or remodelling. When making your inspection, tap and push the panels to see if the builder has skimped. Panellings should be at least 1/4 inch thick and the framing members should be placed no more than sixteen inches apart.

Often a homeowner will finish off a basement recreation room with wood or simulated wood-panelling after moving into a house. The purpose may be entirely decorative or designed to lower heat transmission. To lower heat transmission, it is important that the panels be furred out from the masonry wall to provide an insulating air space or space for insulation. (See Chapter 10.) If this type of panelling is in the basement of a house, it is possible that it was put there to serve as a cover-up for cracks or a damp, leaky basement. Keep your eyes open for other clues.

Condition of paint. In second-hand houses one of the greatest detractions to indoor appearance is peeling or cracking paint. This condition occurs anywhere — around windows, doors, baseboards, walls, or ceilings. Ceilings are particularly unattractive with patches of paint peeling and falling to the floor.

If the paint job in the house you are considering is in bad shape, a careful evaluation of the coats required for a new job should be made. Often a sanding and scraping job is required. It is also possible that a complete renovation of the ceiling surface will be necessary before painting can be done. Professional help is recommended, but a few suggestions given in Chapter 10 may be helpful should you desire to do the work yourself.

In new houses, the prospective buyer should be wary of cheap or chalky paint, insufficient coats, and sloppy workmanship. Make sure that no small patches of paint are left on the window panes.

Most paints are not graffiti-proof. Marks made by children cannot be cleaned off easily. Relatively expensive urethane-base interior paints are available, however, that can save parents many headaches and children a few spankings when they get too ambitious with crayons and pencils.

If you don't like the wallpaper in a prospective house and if it is tight with well-fitted butt joints, the paper surface will make a good base for paint or additional paper. This is particularly true in fifty year old houses that may have much cracked plaster beneath.

A good, but somewhat technical book on interior and exterior paints and other organic coating is *Organic Coatings,* Building Science Series No. 7, prepared by the National Bureau of Standards, Department of Commerce. It can be obtained from the Superintendent of Documents, U.S. Government Printing Office, Washington, D.C., 20402.

Electrical Outlets. While inspecting the walls make a careful check of electrical wall receptacles. Are there enough receptacles? Code requirements vary, but a receptacle every twelve feet is desirable to provide outlets for lamps, accessories and appliances and to preclude the need for long extension cords. Correct plug receptacles have two slots and a round hole, which accepts the plug for the third prong in modern "fail-safe" lead cords. *To be effective this third hole must be connected within the junction box behind the receptacle to a third wire leading to a ground connection at a distant place in the house.* If it is not, you may have a false sense of security and may get a shock when you touch an electrically "hot" window air-conditioner case, electric drill, or metal-cased lamp. One can determine if a ground connection is there by removing the plate on the wall and looking for a third wire connected to the metal-lined hole identified by a green mark. (Warning: *the appropriate circuit breaker or fuse in the main panel box must be disconnected before fooling around under this plate!*) All electrical supply houses and many boating catalogues offer a very simple plug-in tester to determine if the ground wire is connected. One brand widely used is called "Hubble" tester.

Receptacles in old houses have only two holes or slots, and may cause shock unless adapters are used to accept the three-wire plugs. These adaptors, obtainable at hardware and variety stores, have three holes in them with a green pigtail attached to the green-identified hole. The end of this pigtail should be attached to the screw which holds the plate to the metal junction box behind it. *This screw must be in electrical contact to the remote ground connection; otherwise the house residents will be faced with a false security.* A local electrical contractor can be engaged to determine if the screw is grounded and make the proper connection.

Types of switches. Many new houses have silent mercury switches. Houses constructed before 1950 have the type that clicks when a positive connection is made. Both types are efficient and will last for years. Try them for proper connections when you walk through the rooms.

Air leakage through walls and floors. A common fault in poorly constructed houses is air leakage, which places expensive and undue loads on furnaces and air-conditioners. This leakage is difficult to detect. If you are inspecting on a cold and windy day, hold your hand next to a few switches, wall receptacles, wallboards, and shoemolds; you might feel the cold air coming in at these points.

Every house has air leakage through small cracks and door openings, and there are 1/2 to three air changes per hour, depending on construction. A tight house with 1/2 air changes per hour could retain the smell of stale cigarette smoke; a loose house with three air changes puts pressure on the furnace or air-conditioner. Measurement of this change is impossible without expensive professional procedures. You can look for offending cracks, however, near the basement stairway and around windows and doors.

Wall thermostats. A faulty wall thermostat can give trouble if it fails in the middle of a cold winter night. It is suggested that you be leary of the old rectangular, upright thermostat. The newer types are usually round, like a small clock. An added feature of new hot-air thermostats is the control that allows for continuous air circulation whether the heat is on or off.

Thermostats should not be located directly above a radiator or hot air supply duct. They should not be placed on outside walls or near cold drafts. Notice the position, size and type of radiators and heat outlets as you walk from room to room (See Chapter 6.)

Wall insulation. To see whether there is insulation in the walls, take off the covering plate to a switch or receptacle and look for a piece of glass fiber insulation next to the metal junction box. Use a flashlight. (**WARNING:** Remove the appropriate fuse or disconnest circuit breaker first.) If you don't see insulation make inquiries of the sales person or builder.

Good practice dictates about four inches of insulation if glass fiber (R-13) is used in the wall. Some houses have an indeterminate amount of loose mineral wool which is never as satisfactory as the glass fiber material or the rigid foamed polystyrene and solid polyurethane.

Of these two rigid insulating materials, foamed polystyrene is the more popular. It has a higher insulating rating than the corresponding thickness of glass fiber. Often it's placed indoors between the studs and back of the dry wall (with an air space between the wall and the insulation). A 5/8 inch thick drywall (type X) should be used because it is fire retardant, and will provide protection from plastic-generated toxic gas if fire occurs.

Not many builders provide this thickness, but consider anything less then 1/2 inch unsatisfactory.

In some buildings erected after 1970, the foamed polystyrene is used instead of pressed cellulose fiber sheathing. One manufacturer makes a tongue-and-groove type that helps cut down on air leakage to the house. It comes in four by eight foot panels. Taking the place of the cellulose sheathing it would, of course, be outside of the wood framing and studs.

The greatest disadvantage of foamed polystyrene on the outside is its soft consistency; this leads to vulnerability to damage during wall construction, and gives less support than the more rigid pressed cellulose fiber sheathing. It is extremely important that corner bracing of the wall frames, preferably set into the studs, is used.

If the house you are inspecting has the foamed polystyrene on the outside of the framing plus at least R-13 fiber glass insulation in back of the dry wall and between the studs, it will have what is known as a *Superwall*. Because the rigid foamed material on the outside of the wall is unicellular and acts as a vapor barrier, it will not breathe and allow moisture generated in the house to escape to the outdoors. A polyethylene sheet would therefore be nailed to the studs below the drywall to serve as another vapor barrier to keep the fiberglass blanketing from becoming wet and useless. With these two vapor barriers, indoor moisture will be excessive; you will probably never need a humidifier, and you may need a dehumidifier. Two or three exhaust fans in the house to remove moisture would be advisable.

Polyurethane has better insulation qualities than even foamed polystyrene. It is being used more and more these days, and may ultimately be the most popular rigid material.

Brick veneer construction before the energy crisis depended sometimes upon an air space between the veneer and sheathing and upon the properties of pressed cellulose fiber sheathing for insulation. The solid foamed material is now being placed between the veneer and wooden framework greatly lowering heat loss.

Another use of the rigid insulation is sandwich panelling; in

97

this case the foamed stuff is sandwiched between two four by eight foot sheets of wood, one being a finished veneer wood for use on the interior wall. While effective, this panelling poses a problem of toxic fumes in case of fire, because of the high flame-spread rate of the wood veneer.

Insulation of masonry walls. In the 1930's the practice of furring the inside of masonry walls to provide an insulating air space became universal. Most interior walls prior to this date were plastered directly to the back of the masonry wall, and insulation was almost non-existent. You should tap the walls in older masonry houses to see if they are furred; if there is none, you may want to make a furred interior false wall yourself. (See Chapter 10.)

DOORS AND WINDOWS

Doors. Doors are classified by their architectural style, material, and method of opening. For example, you may have a six panel, wood hinged door or a metal flush, four sectional bifold.

As you walk through each room, notice its type of door and how it opens. The conventional hinged doors are the most trouble-free, although space to swing open and close may make a sliding bi-pass or bi-fold (jack-knife) door more suitable. It is unfortunate that bifolds and sliding doors have so often replaced the hinged door on closets. No longer is there space for door-hung shoe racks, tie racks, hanging hooks, and, too often, the clothes you want are in the other half. The cheaper bifolds now installed in new houses tend to jump the track or develop trouble with the pivots. With settling, the sliding door jambs on the bottom floor guide, causing the door to rise up and jump or damage the hanging track and trolley.

The sliding bi-pass doors have an adjustment allowance on the top trolley hanger, and the bifold or jack-knife doors have an adjustment allowance on the bottom pivot. In fairness to these doors, much of their trouble is related to poor workmanship in the original hanging of the door or framing of the opening.

There are several architectural styles of doors. The six-panel, or colonial, and the flush contemporary (usually hollow-core) are the most popular. There are many styles of lock hardware; make sure the bedroom and bath locks have a safety trap from outside to unlock the door in emergencies.

Windows. Windows have been discussed in some detail in Chapter 3. Other window items that you should check are: (1) Do they stick because someone neglected to free them shortly after the paint had dried? (2) Has the putty securing the panes to the mullions and muntins deteriorated and started to break away, so that reglazing is required? (3) Are the sash cords or balance mechanisms in good order? (4) If they are casements or awnings, does the crank system close the window tight? (5) Do the placement and size of the windows allow for proper furniture placement? and (6) Have previous paintings slopped up the glass to the extent that razor scraping is necessary?

THE BATHROOM

The bathroom should get the most thorough inspection of any room in the house, including the kitchen. Many things can go wrong here, and if it is not designed well the homeowner will be subject to inconvenience and constant replacements for years. To start, one requirement is a good ventilating fan for removing odors and excess humidity in the air. Such humidity can be harmful to the walls, paint, paper and insulation. Check for proper operation in air-flow; does the fan force air out of the room?

Beware of an old house with only one bathroom. This will cause family friction and inconvenience, A house with two or three, or one and one-half to three and one-half bathrooms, makes for better living and a higher resale value. A half-bathroom is usually considered a room with a toilet bowl and a wash basin. Check the operation of faucets, toilet bowls and showers in all these bathrooms.

Leaks in the bathroom. The ceilings under bathrooms frequently show evidence of water staining from above. This trouble is usually caused by insufficient or dried-up caulking between the tub and the wall or floor. A tub, sink or toilet has usually over-flowed at least once in any house, and each time it does the water will find a way to the ceiling beneath.

The best prevention against floor leaking is a shower or tub door made of safety glass or plastic. However, sliding doors often jump the track and cause problems.

Ceiling stains beneath the bathroom can be identification of serious and expensive pipe or shower pan repair. Usually when this is the case, the ceiling below will be wet or heavily damaged. The only way to define the cause for sure is to make the following tests:

(1) Direct a hose carefully and directly into the drain opening, so only the drain is being tested. Let the water run for fifteen minutes. If the drain is bad the leak will show up within a half hour on the ceiling below.

(2) Fill the shower base with an inch of water; if necessary stop up the drain to allow the water to build up. You are now testing the lead pan base only; if you want to narrow down the location of the leak, keep the water from the hose directed only around the drain fitting, since the juncture of the drain and lead pan is a logical source of leak. Examine the ceiling below again, as the leaks are small and it takes the water sometime to diffuse through them.

(3) Use the hose again to spray heavily all the walls in the shower or tub. Again, after a wait, examine the ceiling. If it leaks now, only caulking and grouting are required on the tiles within the shower.

(4) To check for valve leaking or pipe section from the valve cut-off to the shower head, turn on hot for a few minutes and observe below, then cold and observe again. You must wait again, of course, after each operation.

(5) Spill water on the floor and observe again. Follow Step 3 instructions. The tub and floor joint, or any tile joint next to something else, needs to be re-caulked or grouted many times.

If a water-supply pipe is leaking upstream from the shut-off valve, the ceiling plaster below will be wet and continually falling down. Tub or tub showers should have a trap door on the wall in back of the spigots; look in here to observe leaks.

If the shower lacks pep and fails to develop a good set of jet streams, but the other plumbing outlets have good pressure, have no worry. The shower head might be adjusted or cleaned into new life, or a new inexpensive showerhead may be installed without the services of a plumber.

Water pressure. Test the water pressure from the faucets to determine the condition of the pipes and to become aware of any inconsistency in low pressure reduction with multiple use. More details on the significance of this are included in Chapter 6.

The toilet. The toilet bowl can be a source of trouble. The mechanism of the tank behind can be in its final stage of life, or there may be a leak in the bowl itself. In checking the tank, look for a downward bend in the rod connecting the float ball to the valve mechanism. This indicates that the owner of the house has temporarily overcome a poorly functioning valve system where the tank fails to fill completely or continues to run. A new tank assembly may soon be needed.

If the tank fails to begin to fill and the water gurgles down the plumbing system, even though the flushing handle is jiggled, replacement by a rubber or plastic tank valve obtainable at any hardware store is probably all that is necessary.

Water around the bottom of the bowl may be caused by a cracked bowl, tank, or pipe fitting, or a loose seal at the floor flange. In the summer it may be due to condensation on the tank or pipes. All are correctable.

When inspecting the tank mechanism, look for a date somewhere near the top of the tank. This date indicates the month and year the tank was manufactured, and will give a good clue as to the age of the house. Many times this will indicate an older house than was represented; if the previous owner has replaced the bowl since the house was built, the date will be meaningless.

The sink. The best bathroom sinks are made of porcelain over cast iron or of vitreous china; there are equal advantages and disadvantages to both. A fancy lavatory is made of vitreous china because of the care of molding during manufacturing. Cheaper porcelain or enamel on steel sinks, which are most popular today, tend to chip but give good service.

Changing the type of lavatories is a favorite bathroom remodelling job. Vanities with cabinets can easily replace old sinks. A one-piece vanity top and bowl of molded plastic resinous materials provides a glamorous marble-looking finish and for reasonable cost.

Tubs and shower stalls. Tubs in the past have been either porcelain on cast iron or porcelain and enameling on steel. Both types are sturdy and last many years. In recent years the fiberglass reinforced polyester tubs, some with integral plastic walls, have come into favor; these also show good promise.

Shower stalls in the past were made on the job with ceramic tile walls and ceramic tile base over a lead pan. Steel showers, common today, sound tinny and rust at the base. Stalls are now manufactured in fiberglass with reinforced polyester walls and base as one integral piece, and are extremely water tight. Precast concrete shower bases are available for use with wall tile or other sheet wall coverings such as formica. These bases eliminate the lead pan.

Tests were performed with fiberglass reinforced polyester under a pilot-testing project; the results are detailed in National Bureau of Standards Building Science Series Report No. 22. They show that fiberglass reinforced polyester's resistance to abrasion, staining solutions, cigarette burns and electric heat is not far behind resistance of the conventional vitreous china fixtures. This report can be purchased from the U.S. Government

Printing Office, Washington, D.C., 20402.

Waterproofed wall covering around the tub and shower are essential to the protection of adjacent walls, floors and ceilings. Ceramic tile applied with cement is probably the most permanent of these coverings; when installed with a mastic or glue application, it is a second best and performance is highly dependent on well-maintained caulking. If water works through the joints, the mastic base may deteriorate.

Plastic tile if installed correctly can give fair protection. The use of tile on walls other than the shower is losing popularity largely because of cost, but also because water resistant wallpapers offer wider decoration themes.

Floor tile of ceramic is more durable than resilient (composition) tiles such as vinyl. Vinyl floors are less expensive and are offered in a wide assortment of colors.

Wall exposure. A bathroom with four interior walls and ventilated with an exhaust fan is much warmer than one with two or more exterior walls, especially if one wall is next to a tub. A person standing in the tub will feel the chill of a cold wall, because heat is radiated to this wall and drains away from the body.

Make tests in the bathroom. Try operating the bathroom devices and watch the drainage. You may feel shy and embarassed about turning on the water and flushing toilets (or trying the burners of the stove when you go into the kitchen). Don't be. The house is your investment, and you will inherit problems unless you detect them prior to purchase. You have every right to inspect and question.

THE KITCHEN

Most buyers will give the kitchen the most thorough check of all and may be influenced more by its decor and efficiency than by any other room of the house. This is good. Inspection *should* be thorough because it is the most expensive area to remodel.

Traditionally the kitchen area has been a popular room for the entire family. Tests made at the University of Illinois a number of years ago to arrive at optimum house layout, resulted in strong confirmation of this — a theory which architects and builders had held to all along. A model house was occupied rent-free by a family, and from time to time, room arrangement was changed by moving the non-load bearing walls while the family was roomed out for free. Purposely, in the rearrangement of rooms, the kitchen was made smaller and smaller, As suspected, the university investigators found that regardless of how small the kitchen became, the family ate their meals and entertained their guests almost exclusively in this room. A small kitchen with its modern appliances can get uncomfortably warm even in winter, however, and there is a lower limit to size.

For inspection purposes kitchen evaluation may be outlined into these 5 categories.

1) Design potential:
   - Is the floor space and size suitable to your needs? If not, can a partition be removed or may it be enlarged and how involved is the change?
   - Openings: Do large windows restrict the placement of cabinets, counters and appliances? Are there multiple doors opening to dining room, hall, basement and outside that make it difficult to work uninterrupted by traffic? Are there means to have large continuous counter space?
   - Is there room for an informal eating area?

2) Layout:
   - Is there counter space on both sides of the sink, the range and next to the refrigerator?
   - Are the arrangement and location of appliances complementary and in reasonable proximity to the working triangle: sink-stove-refrigerator?
   - Is the refrigerator (most used by all family members) away from other work areas, and is it hinged right or left?

3) Cabinets:
   - Are there ample wall cabinets — and with shelves adjustable or large enough to accommodate dried foods?

104

- Are there base cabinets for large pans, some with drawers for utensils? Modern kitchens are many times delinquent in base cabinets.
- What about quality and style of cabinets? Are they to your taste?
4) Appliances:
   No kitchen is now considered modern unless it has:
   - Range, or cooktop with separate oven
   - Fan-hood-light combination
   - Dishwasher
   - Gargage disposal
   - Refrigerator-freezer
5) Testing and judging procedures for appliances:
   - Turning on and cycling through, watching and listening.
   - Judging their expected performance and remaining life by age and brand.

Kitchen location. Kitchens often fit into the floor plan of a house much as the hub of a wheel fits in the spokes. Access is desirable from the kitchen to the front door through the hall, to the dining room, the basement and laundry areas, and to the rear kitchen-stoop and garage. Consistent with this is the recent practice where family rooms and breakfast rooms are designed adjacent to the kitchen. Because of the hub-of-the-wheel pattern and the number of doors that are involved, there is a conflict between an optimum pattern of traffic flow and cabinet space. You, as a buyer, will have to decide on the compromise you can accept.

Convenience and relationship of equipment. A good efficient work area with convenience to tools, counters, machines and storage, means less wasted motion. Doors that open from the range or dishwasher must not block something else that gets high use. The refrigerator should be accessible to all the family, preferably near a door and away from the meal preparation area and stove.

Cabinets and pantry. Style of cabinets is a matter of choice. Metal cabinets of high quality are durable, but cheaper wood cabinets are a better buy than cheap metal ones. Natural wood finishes have had wide acceptance since World War II. Many excellent cabinets are obtainable today with plastic laminate finishes.

It's difficult to have too many cabinets. Every *base* cabinet usually means more counter space above. Small "Bulkhead" cabinets above the normal seven foot high wall cabinets are difficult to use but should be considered when space is at a premium.

People are storing more food these days in anticipation of higher prices due to inflation. Newer homes, consequently, often have pantries; these are great favorites, even discounting the inflation aspect.

Think vertically in a kitchen. In a small kitchen you may see a double oven, burners, and a fan-hood-light fixture all in a twenty-four inch space, and a refrigerator with extra space in height rather than in width. A simple sink, rather than a double sink, coupled with these other space-savers may mean just extra space required to fit in a dishwasher — and a dishwasher means twenty-four inches above available for counter space.

The refrigerator. If the refrigerator is old, look to see if it's well-gasketed at the door. If it's relatively new, determine if it has an automatic ice-cube maker and an automatic defroster. The latter is a big energy consumer and you may not want to pay the energy price. Casters for rolling about are a convenience. Determine the accessibility of the condenser coils for cleaning and improving the efficiency of the appliance; when these coils are on the back of the refrigerator, it is difficult to improve efficiency. A better design is where the coils are in an accessible space underneath. These coils underneath are so confined that they need a fan to draw air through the coils, which brings smoke and grease, which picks up dust. Clean twice a year.

Range and oven

Any stove, if not well-designed or well-maintained by the previous owner, can present problems. With gas fuel the pilot light vents clog and may not respond correctly. Check all burners including the oven. Check the color of the flame, which should be bluish in color; it is not, correct the air mixture by turning a hole-disc in the gas supply near the burner. If electric, turn on all burners at once and listen for a buzzing sound indicating loose connection. Watch for dimming lights in the kitchen, and note how long it takes the burner to heat up.

You should consider the safety factor for children in the stove you are examining. It is generally more difficult for them to turn on the burners in an electric stove than in a gas stove — especially if the on-off switches are placed in the back where they are inaccessible. A convenience outlet on electric ranges for plugging in small appliances can be dangerous. It is often a two wire arrangement without a third wire for connection to ground. Thus, if it has an electric fault, you could receive a lethal shock should you touch the appliance and the stove at the same time.

Some oven doors, because of insufficient insulation and direct conductivity to the outside metal, are difficult to handle when the oven is hot. The pan compartment below the oven in some older models is so hot it's impossible to reach in for a pan. It would be wise to examine the analysis of oven brands in the *Consumer Reports* magazine; this reading habit can apply to the rating of all appliances.

Some stoves have an extra, smaller, oven over the top burners for warming rolls, or cooking a single pie, a few potatoes, or a casserole. This added feature might save heating costs and be convenient for baking, but it makes the space over the back burners dark and difficult to work in. A good up-to-date range should have timing controls for delayed starting, preselected duration and stopping.

Self-cleaning ovens. Many new homes have self-cleaning ovens in kitchen ranges. Some operate constantly over long periods at about 900 degrees, not only using large amounts of energy but also adding to air-conditioning costs in the summer. *Consumer Reports* states that because the self-cleaning oven comes with so much insulation "it isn't necessarily so" that it uses more energy than one you clean yourself. It follows, based on the same argument, that costs for air-conditioning will not be increased by its use. But *some* self-cleaning ovens are not so well insulated. The sad commentary here is that ovens that require manual cleaning should be better insulated. (See this issue of July, 1974, for more information about ranges and self-cleaning ovens.) There are others that have a manual control for operation only when needed. A list of the operating principle of two kinds of self-cleaning ovens is shown below:

(1) The most popular type of self-cleaning oven is the pyrolytic type, which is also called a self-cleaning oven. It uses very high oven temperatures during a heating cycle or cleaning time. During the cycle, the high heat burns up residue of baking grease, pie drippings, and other foods which may have adhered to the side of the oven. The pyrolytic self-cleaning feature is found in both electric and gas ranges; cleaning time consists of about two to four hours, and in some models timing is adjustable.

Consumers' Research, Inc., in their Annual Consumers' Bulletin for 1973, reports that the pyrolytic cycling does "an amazing job". In those oven tested by CR, the oven gradually heated up until it reached a temperature between 900 and 1,000 degrees. The actual cost of fuel during the self-cleaning cycles will be less than ten cents with electricity at 2.1 cents per kilowatt hour, and about half the amount with natural gas at ten cents per therm.

(2) Another type of self-cleaning oven — used principally in gas ranges — is the catalytic or continuous cleaning type. It employs a special coating on the oven liner, which gradually oxidizes the unwanted residue each time the oven is

used at normal baking temperatures. Less energy is required for this cleaner, but there is some evidence to show that the catalytic method of cleaning is not as effective as the pyrolytic method.

Utilization of fuel in a range. About eighty percent of the power supplied to a burner of an electric range is utilized by the pan and its contents during cooking. In contrast, only about forty percent is utilized when gas heating is used. However, gas is cheap enough in most areas of the U.S. to more than make up for this difference and it is therefore usually cheaper to cook with gas.

This difference in efficiency is not as important in the winter as in the summer. If gas with its "wasted" heat is used, it helps heat up the kitchen. In summer, it adds to discomfort and to the load imposed upon the air-conditioning system.

If the house is not properly ventilated by exhaust fans or just plain cracks in the building structure, the wasted gas heat in the winter may contribute to condensation problems, as one of the products of gas combustion is water.

The exhaust fan. An exhaust fan and a hood over the stove, preferably with a light is a must. Look for a grease filter; it will reduce the fire hazard. An increasing number of fans in homes today vent the fumes back into the kitchen after passing lightly over undersized charcoal-and-grease-filters. Discount their effectiveness entirely. Wall fans remote from the range lose approximately fifty percent effectiveness at a five foot distance.

The dishwasher. Most dishwashers on the market are of good quality these days. One poor feature which should be avoided is an arrangement that allows water to pool in the bottom of the washer. Warm water in the dark encourages the growth of bacteria, and if washings are spaced a week apart, the organisms will have a good opportunity to multiply.

An air gap, or device protruding through the wall or countertop, is necessary to prevent the back-up of sewage into the machine in the event of sewer blockage. The device consists of a small open pipe shaped like a shepherd's crook with a metal cap over it. Sewage stoppings cannot back up through the air gap into the machine.

Competitive or "builders' brand" dishwashers, as opposed to top-line brands, can be very high maintenance items after seven to eight years of use, especially in a home with children.

The garbage disposal. Test the garbage grinder and make certain that the water drains out properly. If not, it will back out of the dishwasher air gap. Listen for noise. Run briefly without water; defects will sound louder. Look under the sink, notice wiring, switch location and vibration. If the sink-drains and the trap-return to the wall are at a level near the top of the disposal, back-ups are more likely when the dishwasher is turned on.

Sink faucets. Test the faucet by turning on the hot and cold water. Some faucets leak, drip, or chatter when operating. Don't accept any of these defects. Many modern faucets, although attractive, are difficult to operate and repair, and are not like the old, simple spigot faucets which require only washer replacement. If you have a choice of one of these new swivel single-lever faucets, consult a quality plumber for information on the most trouble-free brand. A spray attachment, or place for spray attachment, is also desirable.

HOUSEHOLD APPLIANCES

The washer and dryer. The design of washers and dryers has stabilized so that the features, cycles of operation, and quality of performance are about all the same regardless of make. Maintenance problems vary but are usually reasonable low if the devices are manufactured by one of the leading companies; reference to a consumers' guide is advisable.

It is possible that either the washer or dryer may vibrate on the floor, or even walk around during operation. To stop this, level the equipment by changing the height of one or two of the legs underneath. These can be adjusted and set permanently with a screw arrangement.

Washing or drying will vary from six pounds to as much as twenty pounds. If information is available on the nameplate of the appliance or the previous owner can tell you, determine the capacity and weigh it against the needs of your family.

Look behind the dryer for a lint catcher. This trapping device will require frequent cleaning to prevent collecting of lint in the ducts of the dryer (which reduces efficiency) and hazard from fire. Some dryers, vented to the outdoors, are not encumbered with the lint problem, but cause some heat loss to the house.

The dryer should be provided with a safety switch so the drum inside cannot operate until the door is closed. To prevent a child from getting trapped inside the drum, the door should be easy to open from the inside.

The metal casings of electric washers and dryers should be grounded. Even if a three-wire cord is used, a second connection to ground offers insurance against a break in the ground connection in the three-wire circuit. (WARNING: A two-wire connection and no grounding connection of any kind offers serious danger because of possible water on the floor.) Gas operated dryers dry clothes quicker and are less expensive to operate; however, the original cost is more. They do not require special venting to remove unburned combustion gases.

The emphasis on energy conservation has brought about some ingenious methods developed by homeowners to divert the dryer exhaust into the house to save heat and produce humidity for winter use. All that is needed is a "Y" tap on the exhaust before venting through the wall and a crude cap of some kind that can be closed or opened depending on the season of the year. A nylon stocking serves as a first class lint filter.

Central vacuum systems. Don't underestimate the value of a well-functioning central vacuum system. If it comes with the house, chalk it up to a high plus. By collecting the dirt in a central location and having the motor away from the living quarters, there is no dust stirred up in the room, maintenance and dust removal problems are lessened, and there is low motor and fan noise. The system is, of course, no better than the size and power of the vacuum motor.

Appliance warranties. When buying a new house, all manufacturers' warranties should be picked up from the builder. Any servicing information that comes with the equipment should be made available. The builder himself may include specific items of his construction in a warranty, or include a general warranty term such as "house to be guaranteed from structural defects and all hardware, etc., to be serviced if found to be defective within one year." (See Chapter 12 for information on home warranties.)

An older house is bought on the basis of "Caveat emptor" — "let the buyer beware". However, a seller might have new appliance warranties, prepaid service contracts, and repair warranties that he could pass on to you.

Typical printed warranties covering the appliance and components of a house are: range and oven; refrigerator; disposal; dishwasher, fan for kitchen, bathrooms, or attic; inter-com equipment; hot water heater; air-conditioner; humidifier; dehumidifier; furnace; bathroom heater; garage door and garage door opener; pull-down stairway; electronic burglar alarm; fire-protection equipment; vacuum system; washer and dryer.

HOUSE FLOOR PLAN

Arrangement of rooms in the house will have a marked effect on your family, especially if you have children. A second floor would offer a haven from these noisy and energetic young people. You may want separate bedrooms for you and the kids, or if you are in the so-called "golden years" you may not want to climb stairs.

A house with both a second floor and a basement may cause problems, because the tools you need for a repair job on the second floor may be in your tool box in the basement. Likewise, you may not like hauling the vacuum cleaner around from floor to floor. Take account of all these considerations to your life styles.

Bedrooms. The first consideration for bedrooms, of course, depends on family size. In-laws living in, or the possibility of an aging parent and live-in practical nurse, children, ages and sex, guests, are all considerations. Regardless of your family needs and living habits, any house, with less than three bedrooms will be penalized on the open market during resale. Exceptions to this would increase with in-town living and areas less conducive to raising families. The master bedroom suite with ample dressing room, sitting room and private bath, is a requirement in a first class in-town house, even at the expense of losing a bedroom elsewhere.

Notice window placement in regard to double or twin bed arrangement; many new project homes are now being built with fewer windows in the bedroom.

Older houses have fewer closets simply because people inventoried fewer clothes. This lack of storage space is a drawback to modern living styles so study the possibility of additional closets; often the big old bedrooms can give up some of their spaciousness for another closet. In most floor plans, particularly the center hall plan, one or two bedrooms may have common walls parallel to the staircase; there is often space in the upper part of the stairwell not interfering with stairway headroom, that can be used as a raised floor closet serving bedrooms on both sides.

The dining room. The history of the dining room is typical of changing attitudes toward what is desirable and acceptable in floor plans. In the 1950's and early 60's, due to long periods of idleness, it was left out of some new homes. Quite often it was incorporated in a living room "L"; the room became an "area". It looked like a good idea, but it didn't work. People wanted this big room with its long polished table for entertaining bosses and for holiday functions with their families and best friends.

Along with the decrease in popularity of the dining room, the kitchens started to become larger, and the dining room smaller—a change which now seems to find general acceptance.

The family room. In this same period the family room began to replace the living room as the family gathering site. Most people like this room and it is featured in new houses. It is most convenient when adjacent to the kitchen and near a secondary entrance from outside.

The recreation room. The recreation room, which is usually left undone by the builder and finished by the homeowner, is often botched with poor workmanship and ersatz material. A poorly finished recreation room would be better left undone in terms of resale. Many basement rooms are finished off beyond their functional capacity; a workroom with many lights, clean painted masonry walls, bare ceiling and brightly painted floor will serve as a hobby, laundry, or tool area better than a finished dark panelled room with falling ceiling tile.

The foyer. A front entrance foyer is a buffer to direct entry into the living room. Access to a rear or side entrance and, if opening into a vestibule of some kind, is referred to as a "mud-room".

6. HEATING AND MECHANICAL EQUIPMENT

ELECTRIC SYSTEM

Current availability. It is important that the house you are considering have the appropriate electric current for its appliances and lights. Otherwise, you will be plagued with current shut-offs during overloads, which might prove dangerous.

Some elementary understanding of electric current is necessary if you are to make a careful evaluation of such availability. This current, called amperes or AMPS, is related to the amount of electricity drawn from the utility company's power line by an appliance and /or light for a period of time.

Some electrical appliances draw more amperes than others. Resistance-heating devices, such as clothes dryers, electric heaters, electric ranges, and electric irons, draw much more electricity during one second than do electric lights and small motors. This accounts for the heavy cords supplying electric energy to them. A large electric motor or air-conditioning compressor also draws heavy currents and requires a heavy cord.

It follows that the amount of amperes drawn by the total house should equal the sum of that drawn by all electrically-operated devices at any one time day or night. This sum will be very small in the middle of the night, and maximum during the day.

A modern house, which is not heated by many resistance elements, should have 150 amperes available for this maximum.

A house heated by electricity with many of these elements should have 300 amperes available. Some fifty-year old houses will have only thirty to sixty amperes available, unless "heavied up" at a later date.

You may have to rewire your new house if you have four or five heavy-duty modern appliances. Suppose you have three big users of electricity: a dryer, a central air-conditioner, and a range-oven, each of which draws thirty or forty amperes. By estimating fifty amperes for each, you will average out the lights and small appliances, and arrive at a reasonable estimate of 150 amperes.

For new houses, the available current can usually be deter-

Fig. 29a. Panel box with circuit breakers (C/B box.)

Courtesy of Sears, Roebuck and Co.

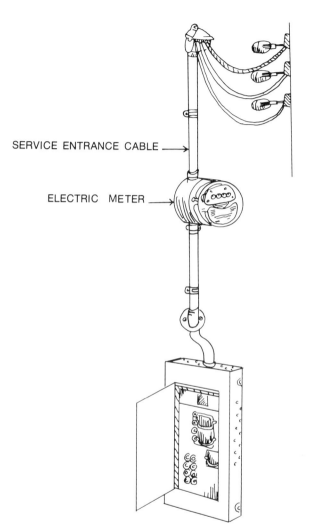

SERVICE ENTRANCE CABLE →

ELECTRIC METER →

Fig. 29b. Panel box with fuses. Service entrance cable, which usually goes through the wall, and electric meter are also shown.

Courtesy of Sears, Roebuck and Co.

mined by reading the current or AMP rating on the door of the electric panel box containing the fuses or circuit-breakers. (The fuse or circuit breaker in this panel box interrupts the flow of current in an overloaded circuit. Fuses burn out and circuit breakers automatically flip a switch.) Occasionally the AMP rating (availability) is placed behind the removable plate cover in the panel box; unless you know what you are doing, *don't take it off*. The rating can also be determined by looking at the heavily insulated service entrance cable outside the house.

The size and designation stamped on service entrance cables will read as in the table below which complies with the National Electric Code. Sizes are arranged from small to large; copper is a better conductor so smaller sizes are used. Exceptions occur because of more effective insulation on some sizes of aluminum wiring.

Available current may be shown neither on the panel box nor service wire in older houses. One can arrive at a good approximation by measuring the diameter of the entrance wire with a wood rule (safer than a metal rule). Most entrance wires in houses built before 1966 will be made of copper, and will have the following dimensions: thirty ampere wire will be circular, and will have a diameter of about 1/2 inch; one hundred, one hundred-fifty and two hundred ampere wires will be flat and oval on two sides, and will have major diameters of one, one and three-eighths and one and five-eighths inches, respectively. If this wire is old and frayed, stay away from it, and make sure a new one is put in!

Both copper and aluminum service entrance wires designed to handle 300 amperes will be in a metal conduit, and current availability cannot be determined from them.

Voltage. Voltage in houses today is usually fused at 110 or 120 volts for small appliances and lights, and 220 or 240 volts for heavy appliances.* Any house not now having 220 volt entry service would be extremely old and obsolete. This voltage is easy to determine by counting the entry wires from the pole: three wires means 220 (two carry 110, and one is a ground).

TABLE 2

Size designation or No.	Available amperage	Available amperage
Small to large diameter	Copper	Aluminum
6	60	60
4	**	**
2	100	100
1	150	125
0	**	**
00(or 2/0)	200	150
0000(or 4/0)	**	200

**These are sizes not commonly manufactured.

*In some geographical areas the two voltages, low and high, because of a special type of connecting circuits used by the utility company will be 120 and 208 volts. The significance of the difference is not great.

A problem that is occuring in most older and some new houses today is low voltage supply. At times of heavy use of electricity in a neighborhood, this voltage can drop down from the normal 120/240 supply, particularly when there is a five-percent "brown-out" by the utility company. This drop can be aggravated by low voltage at the service entrance cable, due to long lines from the transformer on the pole, and by a heavily-loaded panel box. Small-diameter electric lines within the house also are restrictive and cause a voltage drop. In total, at certain periods during the day, especially in these times of energy shortage, the voltage at one or more appliances can be ten percent less than normal, and can be damaging to the appliance. Evidence of this low-voltage supply in the house can be seen by a shortened picture on your television set (two to four inches on each side); while it probably will not hurt the set, it indicates possible low voltage at motor-driven appliances which can be seriously damaged. For this reason turn on a television set and examine the width of the picture when you are inspecting a house.

The problem of continued low voltage can be rectified by pressuring the utility company to increase the voltage to the house and a neighbors' house by installing a transformer on a pole nearer the house. Usually the power company is anxious to know about situations like this because of the possibility of lawsuit; they have no other way of knowing about impending trouble from gradual build-up of air-conditioners or resistance-heating devices in the neighborhood.

Service panel box. This is the junction of the power company's cable and all the branch circuits within the house. (See following section.) Its size determines practical use. Besides containing the safety devices for protecting the wires from overloading, it grounds all wires for the safety of occupants. It may be of either the fuse or breaker type, or a combination of both.

A circuit breaker box (C/B Box) has two distinct advantages over the fuse type box. A circuit breaker can be reset merely by flipping a switch back to the "on" position, provided the situation that caused the overload has been rectified; also there is no chance for the homeowner to overfuse the circuits in the house. Such overfusing may mean a fire because the relatively small wires in the fifteen-ampere circuit will heat up if they have thirty-amperes or more going through them.

Sometimes older fuse boxes make provision for absolute prevention of overload by using special-insert female sockets in the fuse wells. These sockets vary in inner-diameter, and will receive only the size fuse the thread is designed for. They are specific for special *Fustat* fuses of fifteen, twenty, or thirty amperes of blue, orange, or green color, respectively, for easy identification. Safety, of course, presumes that the electrical contractor used the proper sized insert for the branch circuit the fuse is protecting.

Take a quick look at the wires coming from the panel box. In older houses, they will be flexible, accordion-like, metal-clad BX cables, that run across the room either drilled through the joists or secured by plastic or metal fasteners to walls. In newer houses, the wire probably will be plastic-insulated, "Romex-Cable". Any wire that runs outdoors must be of a special plastic type. BX cable is not waterproof unless especially designed. Any house that has less than ten or twelve wires coming out of the service panel probably lacks sufficient circuits for today's demands.

Both fuse and C/B panel boxes have main-cut-offs as back-up safety devices in case the cut-offs in the individual branch circuits fail. In the C/B box, main circuit breakers are placed above all individual switches. The 220 volt appliance circuits often are not routed through the main breaker. In the fuse boxes, large cartridge fuses are provided in place of main breakers. Large appliance circuits will also be protected by cartridge fuses.

The lights and appliances matching individual circuit breakers or fuses should be clearly labelled for quick identification. If not labelled, the time-consuming trial-and-error procedure is required. If you later wish to label you will find that the fuses (or breakers) marked twenty AMP are more apt to go to the kitchen, dining room and basement.

When examining the panel box touch the fuses or breakers to check for heat, indicating current overload. Listen for hum or buzzing sounds, sniff for the odor of burnt bake-o-lite (phenolic) indicating past continuous overload. Be wary of too many thirty AMP fuses. Do not stand on wet floors or have wet shoes when doing this checking.

Branch circuits. A branch circuit is that portion of the wiring system between the outlet (or receptacle) and the fuse or circuit breaker protecting circuits and outlets. This circuit is so named to distinguish it from the primary circuit coming into the house.

Some older houses with copper wiring will have only No. fourteen gauge wire (0.064 inches in diameter for solid wires) in the branch circuits. This is satisfactory for lights, small motors, and window air-conditioners drawing no more than seven and one-half amperes, provided the air-conditioning is not sharing its current supply with other appliances. The National Electric Code now requires larger No. twelve wire for kitchen, laundry room, breakfast and dining room in addition to the No. fourteen wire elsewhere. No. twelve wires should be fused with a twenty AMP C/B or fuse. No. fourteen wire should be fused with no larger than a fifteen AMP fuse. In some new houses electrical contractors use the large No. twelve wire for all circuits. If wiring is of aluminum, one size bigger is required because aluminum is not as good a conductor as copper.

Window air-conditioners in older homes are usually hooked to No. fourteen wires and are not on their own individual circuits. This practice, if overloading is heavy, could be harmful to the machine and may be a fire hazard or cause inconvenience by fuse blowing. Consultation with a qualified electrician is advised, as the situation signifies possible danger.

Window air-conditioners drawing more than seven or eight amperes, and heavy-duty appliances such as range-ovens, dryers, central-air-conditioners, and electric heaters greater than 1500 watts should be supplied by 220 volts. The metal case of heavy-duty appliances near water on basement concrete should be grounded for extra safety even though the modern three-wire system is used.

Aluminum vs. copper wiring. More and more aluminum wiring systems are being installed in houses today. Copper wiring is better, but aluminum wiring is cheaper. Utility companies and electricians are using aluminum almost exclusively for service entrance wires, and an increasing amount of indoor wiring. Unfortunately, electrical receptacles, wall switches, and fuse boxes originally designed for use with copper wiring are not always satisfactory for use with aluminum wiring.

Many receptacles or switches, originally approved by the Underwriters Laboratory, (U.L.) have been suspected of causing fires, and their approval has been withdrawn. These bore the label AL-CU (denoting aluminum and copper). Trouble was suspected at the brass binding screws and plates beneath. Brass is a copper alloy and because of the physical and chemical incompatibility of copper and aluminum, the junctions developed a high electrical resistance, and sometimes fires. The latest U.L. approved receptacles and switches now bear the label CO/ALR.

If the house you are inspecting has aluminum wiring and the receptacles and switches are designed strictly for copper wiring (or of the type labeled AL-CU), check with a local electrical inspector or reputable home inspection service. Some localities allow the AL-CU types with certain very technical modifications.

Because aluminum oxidizes easily, it is imperative that aluminum-copper connections inside the fuse box be covered with an oxidation-inhibiting compound. This contains a powdered metal which maintains a solid connection even though the connections gradually become loosened.

In houses built before 1972, the aluminum wiring was not of good grade and often worked loose from binding screws, causing high resistance and danger of fire. Some precautions are advisable if the AL-CU Switches and receptacles are in the walls, or if the old, poor-grade wire was used. An electrician or a company that specializes in monitoring aluminum circuits and searching for this danger should be engaged. One company that provides this service is the Technical Dynamics Corporation, 550 North Riverside Drive, Crownsville, Md. 21032. Instrutek, Inc., 15 Lincoln Park Center, Annapolis, Md., 21401, markets an instrument for monitoring aluminum circuits.

Be alert to aluminum wire trouble. If, when you are making your inspection, you find that the service entrance cable is hot or even warm, there is trouble. The utility company should be called at once. If there is a trace or smell of smoke at the panel box, a switch, or receptacle, the fire department should be called. Unwarranted static sounds on an AM radio or flickering and dimming lights are danger signals.

Danger of fire in houses with the unapproved switches and receptacles, or the old brittle wire manufactured prior to 1972, may not develop for five to six years. Statistically speaking, aluminum wiring has not caused many fires in the U.S. so far. But make an appraisal of what is in the house and be alert for danger signals.

Safety devices for swimming pools. The National Electric Safety Code now requires a device known as a *ground fault interrupter* for all underwater lighting fixtures in swimming pools. It opens the branch line involved if a conducting path between a faulty light fixture and the ground (the water) is formed. In new homes it should be in all circuits supplying outdoor electric outlets.

THE PLUMBING SYSTEM

This section will discuss the merits and disadvantages of different types of piping and drainage systems, and how to spot trouble and problems peculiar to certain geographical areas. Much plumbing was discussed in Chapter 5, and wells and septic systems will be discussed in Chapter 9. The hot water heater, normally part of the plumbing is discussed in Chapter 6.

Failures in plumbing such as undependable waste drainage and leaking in old pipes can be costly to repair because their replacement usually involves digging up the yard. It is always advisable to inspect carefully and inquire from neighbors or municipal bodies for anything peculiar to that neighborhood, such as frequent stoppage or sewer back-up during heavy rains.

Metal piping. Determine the type of metal piping within the house wherever the water lines are exposed. Are they made of brass, copper, or galvanized steel? Aluminum or stainless steel are more rare.

Since 1935, most houses in the mideastern states have been piped with copper. The trend to copper, brass and more corrosive resistant materials is common in all areas of the U.S. Copper, the most popular of all, has a life of seventy years or more, and takes less labor to install than the galvanized steel pipe it replaced.

Rural areas where wells are installed may have slightly acid water. In these cases the life of the copper is perhaps only 1/3 or 1/2 of its normal life. A quick way to tell galvanized pipe from copper or brass is to look for threaded joints on the galvanized pipe, and soldered joints on the others. Also, copper will not attract a magnet.

Old galvanized piping can present serious problems. If these pipes are approaching forty years in age, remaining life is short; if forty-five to fifty years old, they may be so full of rust that the water pressure reduction, when using more than one spigot, will cause constant annoyance and inconvenience. Also at this age, leaks are numerous.

To test for this deterioration of galvanized pipes, turn on the cold water in the bathroom sink. Then turn on the cold water in the shower or tub, while the sink water is running. If there is significant pressure decrease in the water coming from the sink, it means that pipes are closing down with rust. Do the same thing with the hot water. If the pressure drops more than the drop in the cold water test, the restriction is not in the service line from the street, but within the house, and is probably in the branch line leading to the bathroom.

You should practice this test on several houses. Only when you have developed comparison techniques will the test be meaningful. Visual examination of pipes where exposed, such as in the basement or utility room, may reveal rusty pock marks along the sections of pipe; this is advanced deterioration. If the rusty scabs appear only at the threaded joints, there are still eight to twelve years left.

The branch lines or risers which go up the walls will last about ten years longer than the main line. If replacement is imminent and finances are tight, replace only the main lines, hopefully exposed in the unfinished parts of the house. This will increase pressure throughout. Perhaps the branch lines can wait until a bathroom remodelling job. Never spend money on renovating forty year old bathrooms until all the galvanized piping is replaced.

Plastic piping. Plastic piping is solid like metal piping, but is broken more easily and requires special installation. Prior to 1972, plastic piping was used in most urban areas for wastewater or cold water supply systems in country areas not under municipal jurisdiction. Recently builders have been using this piping in potable, higher-pressure, cold and hot-water systems.

The use of plastic piping is increasing. Based on a survey made by the DE/Journal*, a magazine devoted to news, codes, and standards, some forms of plastic piping, drain waste and vent systems (DWV systems) are allowed by U.S. building codes for all single family homes. The two most widely accepted materials for DWV systems are polyvinyl chloride (PVC) and acrylonitrile-butadiene-styrene (ABS). The survey also pointed out that seventy-six percent of code approvals for single family housing were for PVC and sixty-six percent for ABS — not a large difference.

For the potable, high-pressure *hot-water piping,* chlorinated polyvinyl chloride (CPVC) is used, because its melting point is higher than PVC and just slightly less than the boiling point of

---

*Domestic Engineering/Journal

water (212 degrees). Water in a hot-water heater has a temperature from about 140 to 180 degrees.

Installation of plastic piping requires a special skill, particularly in joining one section to another; consequently, it is imperative than an amateur or an unskilled plumber not be allowed to make the installation.

An underground drain pipe made of plastic will cause less water seepage into the ground than a cast iron pipe — an important property in certain areas where the water drainage is poor. Such a drain pipe, however, may break when a large "rotary snaking" device is used to clean out a stoppage, and should, in some situations, be avoided. All drain pipes regardless of type, should have at least a two percent slope to minimize stoppage.

Plastic pipes inside the house always present the danger of toxic fumes if fire occurs. Gypsum drywall, 5/8 inch thick and with a thirty minute fire retardant rating (Type X) over the piping, will help keep the pipes from igniting if a fire starts inside the house; however, only a few houses will have walls of this thickness. Holes drilled in structural members to accommodate the piping should be closed completely to help prevent the spread of flames and toxic fumes in case of fire; look for open holes when you are inspecting.

Plastic pipes are subject to breakage when exposed, and plastic drain pipes (waste pipes) are very noisy. If you are buying a house during its construction, wrap these plastic drain pipes with insulation to deaden the sound. Use the insulation left over from the walls, and tie with a string and/or jamb between the pipe and studs before the walls are plastered. Remember, though accepted by a growing number of municipalities, this type of piping has not had long years of service to prove the validity of installation techniques.

Clues to past plumbing problems. The following are indications of past problems that may help in evaluating the plumbing system: (1) Recent digging in the yard; (2) The clean-out cap — a large cap with a hex-nut — on the main waste line, which in most houses had never been unscrewed, shows signs of several removals; (3) A main drain that leaves the house above or at the lower floor level may indicate the builder was fighting to obtain proper pitch to the street. Consequently, minimum slope is likely and could result in stoppage; (4) The ground where the sewer goes consists mostly of earth-fill; sometimes the earth settles beneath the pipe, and sags or open joints develop; (5) Turn on several water spigots while you are inspecting the basement and then in a few minutes watch for back-up at the lowest fixture or floor drain.

The water hammer. Water hammer is a noise and chattering which occurs when a valve in a pipe line is closed suddenly. Such noise might occur when a valve closes at the beginning of a new cycle on a washing machine. The phenomenon is caused by a shock wave in the system, and can usually be cured by a plumber who installs a corrective sealed air chamber, or water hammer arrestor.

Frost closure of stack vents. In cold climates such as northern Michigan, Wisconsin, and Montana, determine if the stack vent sticks up too far above the roof and has the correct diameter. Stack vents in below-zero weather will sometimes frost up, close, and allow sewer gas fumes to permeate the living quarters of a house. A number of methods for preventing this frosting are used. The two most common methods are: (1) to use stack vents with diameters of four inches where they go through the roof, and (2) to limit the extent to which the pipe projects above the roof to a maximum of three or four inches. Sometimes insulation of the metal pipe in the attic space is helpful.

For detailed information, write the National Bureau of Standards Center for Building Technology, Washington, D.C. 20234, for a copy of *Building Materials Structure Report,* No. 142, Frost Closure of Roof Vents in Plumbing Systems. Information is also obtainable in the National Plumbing Code Handbook, McGraw Hill Co. See the article by V.T. Manas.

128

HEATING SYSTEMS

Heating systems are usually classified by:
- The *type of fuel* or energy used such as gas, oil, electric, or solar, and by
- The *method of distribution* such as air, water, steam or electric resistance wires.

In the pages that follow, the different types of heating plants are arbitrarily presented, neither by one classification nor another, but by the combinations most commonly in use.

The hot air furnace

The hot-air furnace can be operated by gas, oil, or electricity. The operating life of housing-project furnaces installed since the early '50's is usually not more than twenty-five years, and often less. However, furnaces thirty to forty years of age are still around; the furnaces before World War II were often built heavier and larger.

During operation, this type of furnace heats air which returns from the rooms and then sends it back through ducts to registers, and out again into the rooms. The ducts which bring the air back to the furnace are known as the *return* ducts, and those which supply the air as *supply* ducts. Before the air comes back into the furnace from the return duct, it goes through an air filter where most of the dirt and dust is filtered out to protect the furnace.

In gas or oil furnaces, it is imperative that the air going through the furnace does not come in contact with the flames (or combustion area). The air being warmed travels over a heat exchanger (sometimes known as a fire box) which is heated directly by the flame and which transmits its heat to the moving air on the other side of the heat exchanger. The heat exchanger eventually wears, and cracks are formed; this is what determines the life expectancy of a furnace.

The movement of air through the modern system is accomplished by a blower, a special type of fan which is usually connected to the driving motor by a belt. In older systems, the air is moved by gravity; hot air rises and cold air sinks down. A gravity flow system loses its effectiveness in large homes.

Distribution of air in rooms. In hot-air, hydronic, or steam-heating systems, it is preferable that the registers (grilles), convectors, or radiators be on the outside of the rooms under the windows. The heat rises, forming a moving shield of hot-air over these windows, keeping the windows and walls warm and tempering radiation of heat from your body. A cold surface, such as a cold wall or window, will, by radiation, drain more heat away from a person than a warm surface. A few contractors avoid this placement of room-heating devices because it involves more ductwork.

Return grilles and ducts are essential for proper circulation. The more returns the better. Best location would warrant a return register on an opposite wall from the supply in each room.

In recent years, to save money, builders are placing only one or two returns, centrally located, as in the hall. Under this arrangement there should be at least one for each house level. Bedroom doors must be undercut (one inch air-space at bottom) to allow air to return to the furnace; otherwise, the bedrooms become cold in winter.

Because warm air rises, for hot-air heating it is preferable that the registers be low rather than on the ceiling. The opposite situation obtains for cold, air-conditioned outlets or diffusers. When duct systems are designed for both, a compromise of duct openings will usually favor the cooling system, because cool air is more difficult to handle. If an add-on air-conditioner is attached later to the furnace for summer use and the supply return registers are close to the floor, the unfavorable condition must be tolerated and only partially corrected by directional vents. (The add-on system is discussed in some detail elsewhere in this Chapter.)

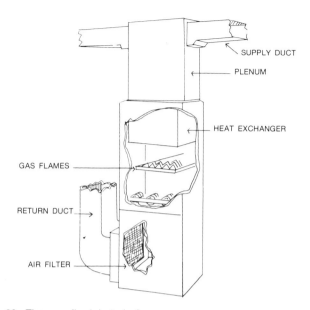

Fig. 30. The gas-fired hot-air furnace.

Courtesy of National Environmental Systems Contractors Association

IF A WATER SYSTEM, WATER IN THE CORE
HEATS & FLOWS THRU PIPES TO THE RADIATORS

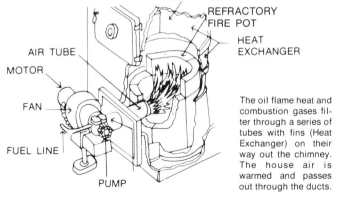

The oil flame heat and combustion gases filter through a series of tubes with fins (Heat Exchanger) on their way out the chimney. The house air is warmed and passes out through the ducts.

Fig. 31. Typical oil-fueled furnace or boiler.

Advantages of the hot-air furnace are:

- No freezing of pipes.
- Very versatile: air can be heated, cooled, dehumidified, humidified, filtered and circulated, all in the same distribution system.
- Quick to respond.
- Low maintenance; no plumbers required.
- Installation price low.
- Less floor or wall space required compared to radiators for water or steam heat.

Disadvantages of hot-air furnaces are:

- The possibility of the products of combustion — the unburned gas or oil, soot and other contaminants — coming through the registers. In the case of gas, this can be very dangerous.
- The heat exchanger (or fire-box) may develop hair-line cracks, and even larger ones, during the years, allowing the unburned gas or unburned oil fumes to get into the air stream. Detection within the furnace heat exchanger by visual means is not easy and many times furnace experts and technicians fail to note it when they look into the furnace with a flashlight. A positive and inexpensive way to spot it is turn the furnace off and paint areas near the burner with oil of wintergreen with a small artist's brush. (A bottle of this oil costs very little in a drug store.) Paint it where the oil will not be consumed by the flame. Then put the furnace cover back on, turn the furnace on, and wash your hands to remove all traces of the wintergreen. Finally, sniff the supply air in all registers. If there is no smell of the wintergreen oil, it is proof-positive that there is no leak in the fire box. The procedure is not practical in a short pre-purchase inspection.
- An electric hot-air furnace does not have this danger. The air passes directly over the heating coils. The coils do burn out, however, much the same as in an electric oven.
- Another disadvantage of hot-air heating is heat cycling. Because the blower operates on an off-and-on basis, the room temperature varies around the room-thermostat-setting from an over-warm to an under-warm condition and back again. In

132

a hot water system, heat remains in the radiators when the boiler cuts off, resulting in more gradual, and lesser, fluctuation of the temperature.

- Sometimes the blower motor is too large, or duct system not properly designed, and the movement of air in the room is uncomfortable.
- Filters need to be changed two or three times per season. Occasional cleaning and oiling is necessary. Overall, there is less maintenance for air furnaces than boilers which supply steam or hot water.

Regardless of hot-air furnace type, keep in mind the normal approximate depreciation schedule for a furnace (twenty to thirty years). Learn approximate replacement costs. The cost of complete replacement of hot-air furnaces is not as expensive as many think, and a furnace giving up the ghost is not the end of the world.

Tests and evaluation of hot-air furnaces:

- Smell and look for black soot and smoke odors around the supply register; these indicate a cracked heat exchanger. A slight general darkening, however, may be caused by dust.
- Cycle through for proper response; shutting on and off is activated by the thermostat.
- Listen for noises, squeaks and fan operation.
- Place a tissue paper in front of the return grille. It should be sucked in and stick to the grille.
- Test the air flow of each supply register by placing your hand in front of the register (holding a cigarette or tissue in front is okay).
- Open and close the damper on each supply register to determine proper operation.
- Note the location of supply and return. Does the air flow across each room or are all the duct outlets and intakes on the inside walls?
- If a central return system, check to see if the doors are un-

dercut an inch or more, so the air can circulate properly.

- Check the connections and condition of the smoke pipe and flue (where the exhaust gases go up the chimney).
- Look for cleanliness and examine general condition of the furnace.
- If oil, notice how quickly and cleanly the fire oil ignites after the burner motor comes on. Delay must not be unreasonably long.
- If oil, look for a service record card tied somewhere to the fittings. This card could give valuable information on past history.
- Look inside the furnace. Things you can learn to judge are signs of heavy soot meaning poor combustion, and condition of the clay brick fire combustion box. On gas furnaces look for rust scale clogging the burners.
- Examine the BTU/hr rating and apply rule of thumb for capacity (see later discussion). Read whatever you can on manufacturers' label; i.e., maker, brand, etc.
- On the outside of the house notice the chimney top. Too much soot and blackness here means wasteful operation or a weak draft. Oil furnaces will stain the upper part of the chimney more than gas furnaces.

Hydronic heating. Boiler is the term used for a heating plant that heats and circulates water; heating by hot water is referred to by engineers as *hydronic heating*. The hot water is heated in a boiler by gas, oil or electricity, but years ago it was heated by coal and wood. From the boiler (equivalent to a furnace), the water travels through pipes, and then (1) to radiators, usually sitting on the floor, (2) recessed wall convectors, (3) baseboard convectors having a copper tube and aluminum fins, (4) baseboard cast iron convectors, or (5) pipes imbedded in the floor, a system often called a radiant heating system.

Water heating systems, although more expensive to install, are considered by engineers and homeowners to be more efficient than a hot-air system. They offer more comfort because the heat is steady and relatively free from cycles; e.g., when a hot-air furnace wall-thermostat shuts off the furnace, the heat stops. With water systems, the heat is retained for a longer time. Unfortunately, the hydronic systems are not readily adaptable to air-conditioning, and are therefore losing favor. If a separately designed air-conditioning system can be installed with ducts, you have the best of both. (See Chapter 6 on air conditioners.)

The average life of a cast-iron boiler is forty years. Any one older than this has since lost its economic value and was probably originally designed for use with a slow, less intense heat such as coal. If it is made of *cast iron*, however, probably the only things that really can go wrong with it are the controls and the wiring mechanism, and they can be replaced very easily. The average life of a *steel* boiler is *much less* because of rusting.

Closed systems. When you inspect the boiler in a new house, you will be surprised at its small size. The pump, or circulator, which sends the water through the radiators or convectors and back again, will be mounted on the lower return pipe at the side of the boiler. On the supply pipe, there will be mounted a water-supply cut-off valve. Near this will be two bell-shaped gadgets for controlling water-pressure and safety. A tank may be visible, strapped to the ceiling. This is an "expansion tank", whose purpose is to allow for expansion of water when it is heated.

Open systems. By *open* is meant that the system is not adaptable to forced circulation, because of an open overflow pipe above the highest radiator or convector. The open system will have no pump or expansion tank.

Many old boilers may be larger and working without a pump and other necessary paraphernalia. This is because the system works by gravity — a much simpler system but slower to respond and prone to heat unevenly. It would not heat well on floors at the same level of the boiler. There is no need for the valve which reduces water pressure, or for a blow off safety valve, because the entire system is open to a small storage tank that has an over-flow pipe in the attic or upper part of the house.

Advantages of hot water heat:
- Less fluctuating of the system, more even temperature.
- Pipes take less space than ductwork.
- Not as much tendency to dry out the air.
- Is quieter.
- No uncomfortable air drafts which occur in the hot air furnace.
- Is usually easier to extend for additions.
- More flexibility to stretch its capacity.

Disadvantages of hot water heat:
- More expensive to install.
- Occupies more floor space (unless pipes are embedded in concrete slab).
- Danger from freezing in uninsulated areas.
- More maintenance required.
- Difficult to adapt to other means of conditioning air, such as ventilating, cooling, humidifying, filtering.

Steam heating. Many steam-heating systems are in existence throughout the country, but they are most common in older and larger homes in the north. In these systems, steam is produced in a boiler and rises in pipes to the radiators in the rooms, not too differently than in the water systems. In some systems, after the steam in the radiator heats the room, it condenses and returns to the boiler as water, in the same pipe through which it came as steam. In other systems, known as two-pipe systems, the steam rises in one pipe and returns as water in another. Heating is more efficient in the two-pipe system.

If you have a two pipe operation, this, if desired, can be adapted to a hot water system. A steam boiler will last as long as a hot water boiler. Advantages of the steam system are more appreciated in large buildings where the length of pipe-run is greater. It heats rapidly and at higher temperatures. Its disadvantages are that it gets too hot, and the radiator often scorches the wallpaper; a young child could get burned on the radiator or pipes. The boiler plant is more costly, and mechanics for servicing are not as readily available. Also there is an inherent danger from high operating pressures.

Electric heating. The electric hot-air furnace, usually consisting of the typical furnace parts with a blower and resistance heaters in the furnace or duct system, is 100 percent efficient; e.g., all of the electric energy supplied to the resistance-heaters in the air-stream gets into the moving air in the form of heat. None goes up the chimney. However, resistance-heating is more expensive to the homeowner than gas or oil heating, and all the claims and boasts of the electric companies about efficiency and cleanliness are blunted by this disadvantage. Electric hot-air furnaces require blower and motor maintenance much the same as the other two types of hot-air furnaces. Electricity is also used to power baseboard convectors, wall heaters, panel heaters, and the boilers of hydronic systems.

Wall-heaters and baseboard heaters. Some houses in temperate geographical areas are heated entirely by separate wall heaters in the various rooms. They are fueled by gas or energized by electricity. According to the American Gas Association, the gas type, which is recessed and placed with face flush to the wall, is dangerous because of the possibility of unburned fumes getting into the room when it has a rated output capacity of over 25,000 BTU/hr. The electric heaters are also recessed and flush to the wall, or can be low and near the floor, in the form of baseboard convectors. The convector types with fins are very much like the convector radiators used for hydronic heating. They usually have enough mass to help damp the heating cycles, and offer a more constant heat than any type of hot-air heat. Some contain water (with anti-freeze solution) as a means for dampening the heating cycles, and are very satisfactory.

Often wall heaters or baseboard heaters will appear in a single room, such as a bathroom, and often are portable. Because there are many variables involved with the gas and electric wall heaters (such as weather conditions, insulation of the house, and size of room), it is difficult to recommend capacity values.

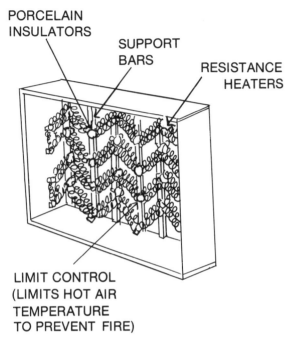

PORCELAIN
INSULATORS

SUPPORT
BARS

RESISTANCE
HEATERS

LIMIT CONTROL
(LIMITS HOT AIR
TEMPERATURE
TO PREVENT FIRE)

Fig. 32. Electric duct heater; used in supply duct for hot-air heating, and also for auxiliary heater in supply duct for heat pump.

Courtesy of National Environmental Systems Contractors Association.

Panel-heating systems. A panel-heating system heats by radiant heat from a large panel, in which are imbedded wire-coils engergized by electricity, or copper tubing coils through which a warm fluid runs. The fluid is usually water. Many people like the heat from panel systems because it does not produce the drafts and fast cycling that hot-air sytems do. The panel can consist of a floor, wall, or ceiling. If the panel is on the floor, it is most comfortable on bare feet.

Because the panel radiates heat to the human body, as heat from a fireplace, the warmth can be cut off by a shield of some kind. In the case of a ceiling panel, the top of a table acts as a shield and a person's feet underneath the table can become cold.

In the case of a floor panel, laid in a concrete slab, it is absolutely imperative that the slab be well insulated from the cold ground with edge insulation; otherwise heating expenses will be enormous. A spring flowers phenomenon will occur in January if bordering the outside walls of the house. This insulation, usually made of foam plastic, sticks down into the earth about eighteen inches. If possible, make sure that the slab has a vapor barrier underneath.

Electric panels of any kind, because they are another type of resistance heating, are expensive to operate. Rooms that have been remodelled, such as an enclosed porch, may use small electrically operated panels on the wall above the baseboard trim of a room, or made up as a baseboard heating unit. They very seldom lose efficiency through the years. Panel heating systems which employ water as the heating medium often lose efficiency because of water leaks and other troubles. If possible, check the system well before you buy a house. A repair job is very expensive. It is possible to purchase dry-wall gypsum panels with electric resistance wires already imbedded in the gypsum material.

For more detailed information about panel heating systems, consult the *Handbook of Fundamentals* of the American Society of Heating, Refrigerating and Air Conditioning Engineers, the 1972 edition. This book can be found in many libraries.

Heating capacities

Capacity of a heating plant is a term describing the heating capability in terms of BTU/hr (BTUH). A comparable *power unit in the metric system is the watt.* The capacity will be marked as input capacity on a heating unit nameplate, visible when removing the front cover. Gas and oil heating units, whether using air or water, will appear to have a capacity in excess of that needed, because the nameplate describes the heating input, and some of this input heat goes up the chimney. Consequently, capacities are usually stated in both input and output, output being the actual usable heat. Hot-air furnaces may refer to output as bonnet capacity. Typical capacities run from about 80,000 to 140,000 BTU/hr input.

In a moderate climate such as that occurring in Washington, D.C., Nashville, Tenn., or Fort Worth, Texas, and for a normally well-insulated house having three bedrooms, 80,000 BTU/hr input is just sufficient. If a house is not well insulated or exposed to high winds in a moderate climate, or even well insulated in a colder climate, 100,000 or 120,000 input may be needed.

A good rule-of-thumb method for estimating capacity needed for a normally insulated house in a moderate climate is: multiply the total floor area of the house by fifty to obtain the input capacity needed. For example, a house with a total of 1600 sq. ft. floor area will require 80,000 BTU/hr input. The above capacities are the manufacturers ratings-input; you will lose at least 20% up the chimney.

These are only estimations but they do offer some guidance for a pre-purchase inspection. Temper the rule with climate and type of house: a rambler, or house with lots of wings and exterior surface, may require more: on the other hand, a simple two-story, square house has less heat loss per sq. ft. of livable area, and may require less.

Capacities on gas hot-air furnaces are more critical than on boilers. Boilers can be made to operate beyond these ratings. Not so with air.

Electric furnaces — hot air or hydronic types — will have lower capacities spelled out in kilowatts or BTU/hr (1 kilowatt equals 3410 BTUH). In a moderate climate, and for a heavily insulated house having three bedrooms, a capacity of about seventeen kilowatts or 58,000 BTU/hr will probably suffice, but the furnace may run constantly. In a colder climate, a poorly insulated or larger house, or a well-insulated house exposed to high winds, electric heat is not practical.

Finally, remember that *all* capacity values are only approximate. A large deviation from them could occur if the house is poorly insulated, unusual in size, or has many cracks for infiltration of cold air.

Fireplaces

Fireplace efficiency depends on design. A poor fireplace is one built into a chimney in the side or end of a house, with three sides exposed to the weather, with a large throat and a flue without an adjustable damper. A low chimney is another poor design feature.

A good fireplace is built inside the house so that most of the heat passing through it, or stored in its brick, is eventually delivered to the house. It has a proper size frontal opening, an adjustable damper so that the warm air lost up the chimney can be limited to that necessary to remove the smoke, and a chimney of reasonable height.

A good ratio of frontal opening to cross sectional area of the flue is seven to one. If the frontal opening is too large, the draft is poor. A cheap way to decrease it is to raise the hearth. Glass doors will eliminate a lazy draft and reduce smoking. Because a fireplace requires a large draft, saving on energy cost is insignificant — and sometimes negative.

For further information on home heating read Farmers Bulletin No. 2235, entitled *Home Heating Systems/Fuels/Controls*. This bulletin can be obtained from the U.S. Government Printing Office, Washington, D.C., 20402.

SOLAR HEATING

The use of solar energy for house heating, at the time of writing, is in the horse-and-buggy stage. Yet some significant developments have taken place and efficient and marketable systems suitable for placement in houses should be available in the next five to ten years.

One promising system, developed at the University of Delaware, employs four by eight panels exposed to the sun at angles from forty-five degrees to vertical position, depending on latitude, system design, and house configuration. These panels contain a gridwork of cadmium sulfide cells backed up by a black surface. To protect the panels from weather, they are covered with glass and are placed on the roof underneath a sheet of transparent and solid plastic material (Plexiglass). When the sunlight strikes the cadmium sulfide cells, electricity which can be used for house lighting is generated. Also, the cells become heated from the sunlight and some of the light passes through the gridwork to a black surface behind the cells which absorbs an additional amount of heat. The heat from the cells, and the heat absorbed on the black surface is, in turn, transferred to the living space by a medium such as air or water.

Excess heat for use at night or on cloudy days is stored in chemicals (eutetic salts) placed in the basement of the house; excess electricity is in storage batteries which placed either outdoors in a shed or in the basement, depending on local codes.

At the present stage of development only eighty percent of house lighting and heating requirements can be supplied at a reasonable price by this type of solar energy. The rest of the energy is supplied by a heat pump powered by current from local utility lines. Since the heat pump heats in the winter and cools in the summer, it is used for air-conditioning during the warm months. It operates in these months predominately during the night hours to freeze a special type of eutetic salt. During the day hours, the heat transferring media — air or water — is circulated through a bank of heat exchangers containing the chemical, extracting "coolness" from it.

TABLE 3
HEAT GAIN, ONE DAY PER MONTH, OVER A PERIOD OF 12 MONTHS FOR DOUBLE STRENGTH (1/8in.) SHEET GLASS PLACED VERTICALLY IN HOUSES, RELATED TO SOLAR POSITION IN FOUR SELECTED NORTHERN LATITUDES

LATITUDE	BTU/hr PER SQ. FOOT OF GLASS				
(DEGREES)	W	SW	S	SE	E
24	11,516	12,795	11,664	12,795	11,516
32	11,056	13,503	13,228	13,503	11,056
40	10,473	14,016	14,636	14,016	10,473
48	9,763	13,997	15,334	13,997	9,763

Data obtained from Handbook of Fundamentals, 1972, American Society of Heating, Refrigerating and Air-Conditioning Engineers

Since the panels are exposed to a harsh, heated, and sometimes wet environment, and since the behavior of the transparent, framing and supporting materials during exposure is not well known, they cannot be considered ready for sale on today's market. The prospective buyer of a house should be wary of the cadmium sulfide panels until there is evidence that all the bugs have been removed from them.

Nevertheless, the panel promises to be useful in the next few years, not only for roof and wall energy collecting surfaces, but also in walls apart from the house such as garage roofs and wind-break walls. These heat-collecting exterior walls could be used for heating hot water and for partial generation of electricity.

A more primitive system, actually in use in some houses today, partially heats a home by means of circulating water that runs down grooves in corrugated metal on a sloping roof. This system is highly publicized in newspapers and magazines, and kits with instructions are being sold to do-it-yourselfers. Despite their simplicity and initial success, there are problems with the system.

When buying or building a house, consider the possibility of allowing for later adaptation of a solar system using the cadmium sulfide panels, the running-water-on-corrugated-metal system, or another system which may be developed in the near future.

Of first consideration for later adaptation is the house orientation. Table 3 will be helpful in determining optimum orientation. Note that southwestern, southern, and southeastern exposures are best.

Although the table lists heat gains for vertical glass (at different latitudes), it gives good comparative values that would also be useful for houses with roofs having slopes of forty-five degrees or more.

The table, of course, will be directly useful for vertical panels. Surprisingly, calculations have shown that the heat gained when the panels are vertical is not significantly less that when mounted on a forty-five degree angle. Each latitude has a optimum angle of roof slope, however, and if the house designer wishes to employ as much of the sun's energy as possible, he must look to an engineering source other than the table.

The style of the house is another significant variable. A salt-box Cape Cod structure as shown in figure 13 is one architectural style that may be pleasing to the homeowner and his neighbors.

A number of promising assemblies which can be placed on rooftops to supply partial energy for space heating, hot water heating and cooking have appeared on the market. Not enough time has elapsed to evaluate these assemblies accurately.

The heat pump appears to be destined to play an important role in solar heating. Since during normal operation, it makes use of small amounts of heat in the outdoor air or in natural water reservoirs, it could, with engineering development, profit even more from heat harvested from sunlight and stored at even higher temperatures. The same heat pump could be used for cooling with a coefficient of performance of about two; this is done at the University of Delaware's experimental house, where it is operated from utility power lines.

Another development in the solar energy field is the large banks of solar collectors; these could be used in common by communities or power companies for generating electricity. Cells for converting sunlight to electricity are only about 10 percent efficient today, however.

THE HOTWATER HEATER

The hotwater heater is an insulated storage tank supplying hot water for washing and other uses. The water may be heated by any fuel — gas, oil or electricity.

The capacity of a hotwater heater is described as the amount of water the tank will hold and the time in which it will make more hot water. Storage capacities, when fired by gas, normally range from thirty gallons for apartments to fifty gallons for large houses. Electric hotwater heaters will have a much greater storage capacity because their recovery rate is low. Because of this low recovery rate, in actual use an eighty gallon electric heater is roughly equivalent to a fifty gallon gas heater.

Recovering rates of the three types of heaters will vary. A typical gas hotwater heater of forty gallon storage size will recover about thirty gallons per hour. This means that the temperature of thirty gallons of water will rise 100 degrees in one hour. The better gas heaters will recover 100% of storage capacity in an hour, in which case storage capacity may be relatively small. On the other hand, electric hotwater heaters recover so slowly that you won't even find the recovery rate stamped on the name plate! There is no such thing as rapid recovery with electric hotwater heaters; oil heaters have a very rapid recovery rate.

Gas-fired hotwater heaters. A good rule for estimating required size of gas hotwater heaters:

> Thirty gal. for family of three
> Forty gal. for family of four
> Fifty gal. for family of five

This assumes normal washing machines, dishwashers, etc. Electric hotwater heaters must be nearly double this, and oil heaters could be less.

In view of the energy crisis, there might be some savings in utilizing a tank of smaller storage capacity and more rapid recovery. There is no sense in storing a lot of water all night long that will lose heat to the surrounding area.

Used widely, the gas-fired hotwater heaters are cheap and efficient. However, they do require a flue for exhaust gas as does a furnace. Gas heaters are now available with a flame of varying intensity to raise the temperature quickly, and the flame subsides to maintain the temperature during the night or when not being used. The variable flame minimizes the need for large storage capacity because recovery is quicker and the owner does not pay so much to store the water all night.

Electric hotwater heaters. Most electric hotwater heaters have two 4500 watt heating elements within the tank, coming on alternatively — *never* at the same time. The two heating elements evenly maintain and increase the heat recovery. The electric hotwater heater is more expensive to operate than the other two types, but a great advantage is that no flue is required.

Placement within the house is only limited by space to place it. Water lines and a 220 volt electric circuit are needed, but there is no worry about gas lines.

Oil-fired hotwater heaters. Occasionally where there is no gas and the cost of electricity is high, an oil heater will be used. This heater has extremely rapid recovery — over 100% of storage capacity in one hour. It is good for a large house, even a hotel. It requires a flue, and installation expense is higher than for gas or electric heaters.

Summer-winter hook-up with oil-fired boiler. A type of hotwater storage commonly found with oil-fired boilers used for house heat, is a system called summer-winter hook-up. It is hooked into the main line of the house heating plant, and a coil through which a separate water supply flows is placed inside the boiler. When you turn on the hot-water spigot, water flows through the coil and is heated almost instantly.

Although initial installation of one of these systems is less expensive than a gas or electric hotwater heater, they are wasteful if used in the summer when no house heat is needed. In these days of energy shortage, use of these devices is definitely out. Other disadvantages include low storage capacity and an annoying drop in pressure when more than one spigot is turned on at a time.

Deterioration of hotwater heaters. Nearly all hotwater heaters today are glass lined to inhibit deterioration and promote longer life. Normal depreciation schedule of a typical residential heater is about ten years. Guarantees are pro-rated up to ten years, which is an indication of quality. Just recently, shorter limits were placed on warranties. There are many hotwater heaters on the market today with only a one year warranty; be on guard for this kind of shortchanging.

How to inspect and evaluate hotwater heaters:

- Try to determine the age. Look for a gas company tag or plumber installation tag. Age is the main depreciating factor.
- The brass fittings at the top of the tank will build up deposits of corrosion (oxides) where connected to the pipes. Heavier deposits indicate age.
- Rust spots at the seams are undesirable. In a gas unit, the amount of use can often be detected by deposits of rust scale under the tank.
- Examine the burners to see if they are clogged; they can be seen if you turn off the flame and use a flashlight.
- A temperature-setting device, usually visible on the side and near the bottom of the tank, should be examined. If the setting is as high as it will go, the heater and tank have been worked hard — a shorter life is indicated.
- Undersize hotwater heaters do not last as long as an adequately sized heater.
- Note the number of appliances using hot water and find out how many people lived in the house. Heavy use means shorter life.
- Look for a local pipe cut-off. The water heater should have cut-off to use when leaks develop.
- An emergency blow off valve should be connected to the pipe or on the heater itself.
- A gas-fired water heater must be connected by a flue to a chimney. Building codes in your area may require a larger flue for a larger heater, because the volume of waste (unburned gas) is more. If electric, a larger electric line may be mandatory.
- Look to see if the water lines are connected correctly. Surprisingly, about one out of ten today are connected with the hot and cold water lines reversed. Efficiency is cut down this way.

AIR-CONDITIONING

Electric central air-conditioning. The electric central air-conditioning system is the most popular type of cooling system in the United States. The most common within this variety is the system where the evaporator (an A-coil shaped like a tent), or evaporating unit, is indoors and the condenser, or condensing unit, is outdoors. The furnace plenum, made of sheet metal, covers the evaporator. It is the central collècting chamber for the conditioned air (warm or cold) leaving the furnace. In heating practice, it is often called the bonnet. From this chamber, the ducts take off to the different rooms in the house.

In all electric-operated central systems, the evaporator and the condenser are connected by copper refrigerant lines, one insulated and the other not. These lines transfer the heat, which is extracted from the air by the evaporator, to the condenser, where the heat is rejected to the outdoors. The refrigerant is often called by the tradename *Freon*. Another, but less well-known refrigerant is *Genitron*. Either one may be designated with a number and the prefix F; i.e., F22.

The evaporator effects the transfer of heat to the outdoors. The refrigerant travels through coil shaped copper tubes, called an A coil. These coils reach a temperature of about fifty degrees, a temperature significantly lower than room temperature, and cool enough to collect water from the humid, summer air. An air-conditioner, therefore, not only serves to cool the indoor air, but also dehumidifies it — contributing greatly to comfort.

Distribution of the cool air from around the evaporator coils to the rooms of the house is accomplished by the blower, used in the furnace for heating in wintertime. This forces the air through the furnace ducts and out through the diffusers, or registers. From the evaporator, a condensate line (a long and straight copper tubing) runs from a drip-pan underneath the cold coils to a drain of some sort. Its function is to remove the water collected on the coils, which is constantly dripping downward into the pan. Plastic drain lines are sometimes used. Look for kinks in

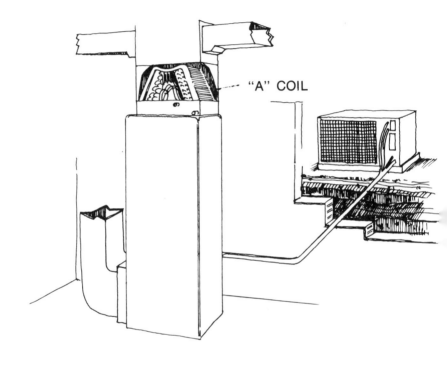

"A" COIL

Fig. 33. Evaporator "A" coil is placed in the furnace plenum for use in summer air-conditioning.

Courtesy of National Environmental Systems Contractors Association.

the line which could cause stoppage.

The condenser (outdoors), a cubed-shaped or cylindrical-shaped unit, contains copper coils which get hot, and a fan which blows the hot air over the coils away to the surrounding environment. It also contains the compressor — the heart of the entire system — which pumps the refrigerant through the coils of the two units, and the refrigerant lines between them. The compressor also serves the very important function of compressing the refrigerant from a gaseous state, to a liquid.

Problems with electrical systems.
Compressor difficulties. The electric central air-conditioning system has unique problems of its own. For various reasons, there are more things that seem to go wrong with it than with a furnace. One of the most prevalent of these problems is compressor failure, although electric systems installed since 1970 seem to be freer of this trouble than those installed before. Guarantees and warranties nearly always give five-year protection for parts on this element.

A quick but cursory test for compressor operation is to turn on the system at the room thermostat. If hot air is coming out of the outdoor condenser, and cool air out of the evaporator, you are all right. A word of caution for making this test in the winter — some manufacturers do not recommend turning on their system when the temperature is below sixty degrees.

Frosting or icing. Another common problem, especially with older systems, is frosting or icing of the fins on the face of the indoor evaporator. The fins are small, razor-like metal plates that surround the copper coils of this unit which give the facing the appearance of a honeycomb.

Frosting or icing, particularly icing, can cut efficiency down markedly. Both are caused either by a blockage of the air-stream that passes across the coils and their fins, or by a shortage of refrigerant. The undesirable phenomenon is more likely to occur on rainy or cool days in the spring or fall.

You can spot trouble by operating the system for about thirty minutes and making a visual check of the evaporator in the plenum, preferably on a cool day. If the system is old, the icing may be caused by a blockage of the air-stream, and changing a very dirty air-filter may help. If that doesn't work, check for an accumulation of lint, dust and grease on the evaporator coils. (Access to the evaporator coils may require a service man.) A shortage of refrigerant will show the same symptoms. The last is the most common cause. A very small amount of frosting on the fins may be tolerated.

Difficulties from noise. Internal noise is a frequent problem in electric systems. Such noise can be caused by a broken bearing or a bent shaft in the blower; a loose belt between the blower and the motor driving; or a too-large motor causing excessive air-movement. If the evaporator is installed in the furnace plenum, as it is in most systems, blower trouble will cause difficulty in the winter months as well.

Indoor noise is most often the result of vibration of the evaporator fan units, its component parts (including the refrigerant lines) and even the ductwork. Sometimes vibration can be cured by adding extra weight to the vibrating parts or by securing them to something solid that doesn't vibrate. Noise from vibration in the evaporator fan unit is often transmitted along the ductwork. The ductwork should always be connected to the furnace plenum by means of a flexible connecting sleeve, made of heavy, closely-woven, treated or non-combustible fabric cloth.

The indoor evaporator unit, whether installed in a furnace plenum or not, should be placed as far as possible from the living quarters. An acceptable sound level in a room where occupants are active, such as a kitchen, may be objectionable in a room such as a bedroom, where occupants are inactive. When possible, it is best to have a buffer zone between the equipment and quiet areas.

Noise in the compressor-condensing unit outdoors has caused many a strained relation between neighbors—even fights reaching Donnybrook proportions. For this reason, when you turn the air-conditioner on during inspection, listen for undesirable noise while you are standing next to the neighbor's house. Put yourself in his position and determine if you would be sore at that new guy who just moved in next door. Further, it wouldn't hurt to listen to the neighbor's outdoor unit.

A common cause of noise in the outdoor unit is the wrong fan in the right unit. If the unit was manufactured by a reputable firm, you may be able to get it fixed. Bearing or fanshaft trouble is also a possibility.

Nearly all condensing units are mounted on concrete blocks. Normally the mass of the concrete is great enough so that vibration isolators are not needed; but for the best results they should be used.

There are times when the unit may remain noisy regardless of what is done to the mounting or parts of the unit. In these cases, homeowners try remedies ranging from fences to walls—usually to no avail because sound turns corners and travels around walls or over them.

Good and bad installation techniques. Poor installation practices (indoors) should take most of the blame for cooling losses in air-conditioning systems. The worst and most common offense is installation of the evaporator in the attic—where temperatures approach 140 degrees on hot days—without following well-established precautions against heat loss.

Sometimes attic installation is necessary. A case in point is a home where a hydronic heating system which has no hot-air ducts is used. Special ductwork, made of metal or elephant-trunk (glass-fiber material), is brought down from the attic to supply cooled air to the rooms below. If this system is used, it is imperative that any metal ductwork in the attic be well insulated to prevent cooling loss. At least 2 inches of R-7 fiberglass material is recommended. It is also helpful if the evaporator itself is insulated. Furthermore, the insulation around the metal ducts or the evaporator must also be protected with a vapor barrier material, to preclude moisture from condensing out of the hot humid air and causing damage to the structural elements below. The vapor barrier must be placed on the outside of the insulation.

An evaporator installed in the attic must have a 4 or 5 inch deep drip pan below it to catch overflow, should the condensate line become plugged. In attic installations, this condensate line normally empties the water collecting on the 50-degree coils of the unit into a gutter or downspout very close to it. These gutters or downspouts can become clogged with leaves.

Since about 1970, metal ductwork with insulation and vapor barrier inside of it is being used for attic installations. You can determine if metal ducts are protected this way by touching them with your hand while the system is operating. They should not feel very cold to the touch.

A common installation defect is poorly-joined ductwork. Builders have been known to leave large gaps in supply or return ducts, causing a large loss of cooled air. This defect results in increased costs and contributes to the energy shortage.

The central gas-absorption system. The gas-operated air-conditioning system, which has an indoor and outdoor unit, works on a different principle than the central electric air-conditioner. It has fewer moving parts and doesn't need the compressor. Cooling is accomplished by the evaporation of liquid such as ammonia. The conditioner requires a small flame to separate the ammonia from a solution of ammonia and water.

In the gas system, the indoor unit operates under high pressure of as much as 300lbs per square inch, a pressure which can cause leaks. However, because of hermetic sealing and good quality-control at the factories, this pressure problem does not seem to be a factor in today's market.

Comparison of gas system with electric system. For a number of complicated reasons, some technical authorities believe that the general efficiency of the gas system is not much less than that of the electric system. Consequently, the choice should be based largely on economic considerations.

The first of these considerations is initial cost. The gas system is generally more expensive in this respect.

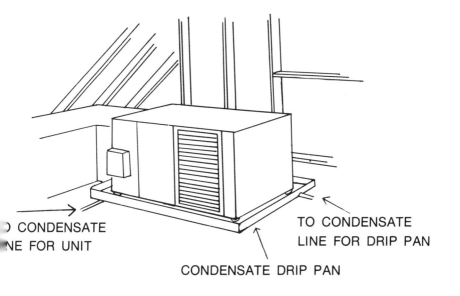

CONDENSATE
LINE FOR UNIT

TO CONDENSATE
LINE FOR DRIP PAN

CONDENSATE DRIP PAN

Fig. 34. An indoor unit (or air handler) for a summer air conditioner or a heat pump must have a drip pan underneath deep enough to hold the condensate water accumulated should the condensate line become plugged. About 4 or 5 inches in depth is usually sufficient. Especially true for attics.

155

The second factor is maintenance. The gas system has fewer moving parts, no compressor, and although it has electric blowers or fans, similar to those in the electric system, cost of fan operation is relatively inexpensive. The gas system seems superior in this respect.

The third aspect is operating cost. The electric system is generally cheaper. Today, gas companies in many cities offer a rate differential in the summer months, — but energy crisis may eliminate this compensatory program.

Both types of systems seem to carry good guarantee policies.

The add-on central system. Older homes with hot air heat often make use of the ductwork and fans to add on a central cooling system. Such a system can be very satisfactory but often there are shortcomings.

It can be electric or gas. In both systems, evaporator cooling coils, or A-coils, fit neatly into the plenum of the furnace in the same way as in a newly purchased system. The blower of the furnace blows air to be cooled over these coils, through the ductwork and out into the rooms. In an electric add-on system, a refrigerant runs through the coils. In a gas system, a secondary coolant coming from an indoor unit goes through the coils.

Because the *difference in temperature* between the air in the supply and return ducts is not the same for heating as for cooling, blower motors of different sizes should be used for the two operations. A larger motor is needed for summer air-conditioning than for heating in the winter. The smaller original motor, often 1/4 horsepower, is replaced with a 1/3 or 1/2 horsepower motor. One compromise motor is often used, however, and each operation suffers some. An adjustable speed motor, with two speeds, is a partial remedy.

Although the problem exists for newly installed electric central systems, it is more serious often in the add-on system, because the installer either retains a motor that is too small or substitutes a motor that is too large. If the motor is too small, the upstairs rooms may not be cooled sufficiently. If it is too large, there will be too great an air flow for comfort coming from the registers. Also, some noise may result from the high flow of air.

Capacities of central systems. A normal and well-insulated house will require about 12,000 BTU/hr (1 ton) for every 500-600 square feet of floor area. If the per ton capacity calculation for the installed conditioner works out to 700 or 800 square feet, instead of 500 square feet, you are in trouble. Trees and overhangs, however, can make a difference. A small house could typically have a total of 2½ tons. Most 1500 sq-ft houses have about three tons; and five or six bedroom houses usually have four tons.

To determine capacity, look on the name plate on the side of the condenser. The model number often has a series of numbers, such as "A-4260" meaning 42,600 BTU/hr. (or a 3½ ton unit). The electric air-conditioning system will average around 7 AMPS per ton in residential sizes. "AMPS" are stamped under a heading "F.L.A.", (full-load AMP). For example, "21.5 AMP", indicates approximately a three ton unit.

Get in the practice of reading these labels and you will soon derive some comparisons.

Window units and units installed through the wall. Even though three to four window units may cool a house satisfactorily, they do not add to the resale value as the central air-conditioner does.

The window unit operates on the same principle as the electric central air-conditioner, with an evaporator and a condenser, refrigerant lines, coils, and a compressor, although it comes in one small package. However, the amount of cooling per watt-hour of energy is less than in the larger system.

One would expect, therefore, that a house with window units would cost more to cool than one with a central conditioner. It would, if the same degree of comfort were obtained. In actual practice, people with window units usually keep them turned off in their bedrooms during the day, and tolerate some rooms *without any cooling at all*. Areas remote from the conditioner never benefit materially from the cold air coming from the unit.

Distribution is never as good as for a central system. It is obvious that window units provide less comfort for approximately the same cost.

Some window units are installed through the wall instead of in windows. Such an arrangement gets around the problems of dirt between the permanently closed windows and ugly installation strips at the top of the space between the windows.

Units can be oversized in a small bedroom and cause real discomfort in the middle of the night. A 6000 BTU/hr. job is maximum for a small room. Regardless of size, a bedroom unit should be equipped with a thermostat to control temperature. To conserve energy and insure comfort, a timer which shuts the entire device off in the middle of the night is advisable.

In many homes, very large window and through-the-wall units are used to cool two or three rooms. The large flow of cold air issuing from these can be uncomfortable when you are close to the air grille. A close approximation to cooling distribution comfort, can be obtained by installing a window unit in the upstairs hall. The halls and stairs serve as the ducts.

For additional information on window units see the July 1974 issue of Consumer Reports.

The heat pump

In the 1950's, when the popularity of air-conditioning was rising sharply, an old principle, known by scientists for years, was harnessed so that the same equipment used for cooling could be used for heating. This principle stated that the outdoor unit, if certain rather simple adjustments were made, could, in the summer, reject the undesirable heat to the outdoors, and in the winter, accept the heat taken from the outdoor air and transfer it to the house to warm it. The principal adjustment involved was a change in direction of refrigerant flow in the refrigerant lines. This change was accomplished with the use of special reversing valves that are triggered automatically by the wall thermostat in the house when the house temperature reached a pre-set level such as seventy degrees.

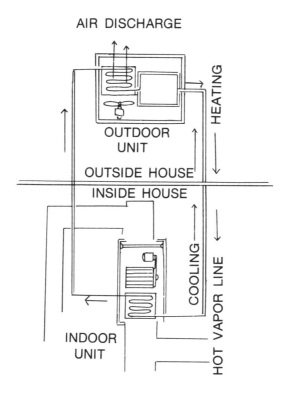

AIR DISCHARGE

OUTDOOR
UNIT

OUTSIDE HOUSE

INSIDE HOUSE

HEATING

COOLING

HOT VAPOR LINE

INDOOR
UNIT

Fig. 35. Schematic drawing showing direction of refrigerant flow in heat pump. For summer operation the hot refrigerant vapor flows to the outdoor unit where the heat escapes to the surrounding air. For winter operation the hot vapor picked up in the outdoor unit flows to the indoor unit where it is used to heat the house.

159

On first thought it appears that the scheme is infeasible and that there is not enough heat in outdoor air to be of much good for heating a house. Surprisingly, there is, if the temperature is above about thirty degrees; even more, if fifty degrees; and almost enough, if it is down to about twenty degrees. Air at any temperature has some heat and this heat can be extracted.

The heat pump became popular in the 50's, particularly in the southern states, because one single system, without a furnace, was all that was necessary to produce year-round comfort. Another factor in its popularity was the sudden advent of wonder stories in magazines and newspapers about a magic "coefficient of performance" (C.O.P.) of the device. According to the C.O.P., the amount of heat taken into the house was two to five times the amount of heat, translated from electrical units (from kilowatt-hours to BTU), supplied by the electric utility lines.

We now know better about this C.O.P. Only theoretically are these large gains possible. In actual performance, this coefficient is nearer 1.5 and 2, depending on the outdoor temperature, the workmanship involved, and design features of the pump itself. Sometimes if there are big leaks in the ducts, the C.O.P. will be even less than one on moderately cold days. Resistance heating with a C.O.P. of one could have been used just as well!

In states like Florida, Alabama, South Carolina, and Texas, where temperatures during many days during the winter are from thirty to fifty degrees, it has become an economical and practical device. Under certain conditions it is practical in states somewhat further north. More and more engineers are looking at its possibilities these days of acute energy shortages.

All heat pumps have electric resistance heaters, known as auxiliary or strip heaters, installed in them which are turned on automatically when the pump itself cannot supply enough heat to keep the house at the temperature set on the indoor thermostat. Usually the heaters are energized in two stages, with the second stage used only in extremely cold weather.

Split-type air-to-air heat pump: The heat pump described is known as the air-to-air heat pump because heat is taken from the outdoor air and circulated around the house by indoor air. The typical pump of this type, known as the split type, has an outdoor unit, mounted on a block of concrete, that has the exact appearance as the outdoor unit used in the summer air-conditioning system. (Only it cannot be called a condenser because in the winter it acts as an evaporator which absorbs heat). The indoor unit is usually cubical in shape and can be installed in a utility closet, basement or attic. Attic installation is not recommended, however, unless absolutely necessary, because temperatures in this space become too low in winter and too high in summer.

Integral air-to-air type heat pump: In this category, the indoor and outdoor units are mounted close together in an area near both the living quarters and the outdoors — such as a utility closet.

The water-to-air type of heat pump: Pumps other than the air-to-air type are infrequently used for residential purposes. The most popular among them is the water-to-air heat pump, where heat is taken from the water in ponds or wells through submerged copper coils. Since water in wells remains constantly at about a fifty degree level, and water in ponds never gets below thirty-two degrees, the seasonal C.O.P. is always more than for the air-to-air system. It is difficult to keep the submerged coils clean in water-to-air pumps.

Problems with air-to-air heat pumps. Heat pump systems have many of the same problems that occur with normal air conditioning systems. It is recommended, therefore, that a prospective buyer familiarize himself or herself with the defects in equipment and in installations outlined in the section on summer air-conditioning.

The devices have other problems of their own, too, some of them extremely bothersome and difficult to resolve:

Difficulties from noise. Noise in the indoor unit can cause difficulty, particularly if the unit is installed in the attic. Being installed separately and not within a furnace, this unit can rattle around, shake and vibrate if installation was careless. Noise in

161

the outdoor unit can cause as much difficulty with the neighbors as that in conventional summer systems. Only more, in fact, since it operates year-round; it changes operation all night long with defrosting during winter.

Failure of auxiliary heaters to operate. A common cause of insufficient heating and the discomfort to occupants in cold weather below thirty degrees, is failure of the auxiliary electric resistance heaters in the indoor unit to cut in when the room temperature becomes cold. Sometimes the first stage cuts in and not the second. The trouble may be in the room thermostat which has the multiple job of (1) regulating room temperature, (2) reversing cooling to heating operation and vice versa, and (3) cutting the electric heaters in and out. The trouble also may be due to the inoperative heater itself.

Defrosting problems. The outdoor unit in the air-to-air system has a defrosting device which frequently causes trouble. Its purpose is to melt snow or ice that forms on its metal fins when heavy moisture and low temperatures occur. Such a build-up seriously impairs efficiency. During normal operation, before this occurs, the pressure in the coils builds up to a point where the defrosting device reverses operation temporarily and the system becomes a summer air-conditioner, heating the coils of the outdoor unit, and, as a result, the honeycomb assembly of metal fins. This reversed operation is short in duration and disturbs the air in the rooms of the house only a minor amount. One way for the prospective buyer to see if the defrosting device works is to artifically build up pressure at the face of the unit, where ice would form, with a piece of cardboard. Then take it away.

Some systems accomplish defrosting by a timing device that automatically changes the system over to cooling operation periodically, regardless of moisture and temperature conditions. This system offers less trouble.

The outdoor unit may become permanently clogged with ice, snow or leaves, but it contains high and low pressure control devices that shut the unit down when malfunction occurs. Unfortunately, these devices themselves often fail, detracting from the heat pump's many good points.

Problems with integral systems. In integral systems, ducts from the indoor unit to the interior of the house must be well-insulated, and there must be no air-change between the two units. Cold air discharged from the outdoor unit during winter can seriously impair efficiency of the indoor unit if the two units are not well isolated from each other — and vice-versa; hot air from the unit in summer would be harmful.

Carefully check operation of old heat pumps. A heat pump installed before 1972 may cause problems, especially compressor failure. The newer pumps, however, generally operate efficiently and have about the same record of maintenance costs as the central electric air-conditioners.

Successful heat pump operation. Despite past problems, the heat pump has served many a home efficiently and faithfully. The two greatest factors contributing to successful operation are: (1) a reputable manufacturer and (2) geographical location. In southern states where many of the days in the winter are thirty to fifty degrees, it really pays. Installation in homes in states like Pennsylvania, Illinois or Michigan is extremely dubious; cost and energy benefits will be no greater than those of straight electrical heat and heavy snows and icy conditions will seriously tax the heat pump.

Additional information on heat pumps can be found in the following bulletin:

> *Heat Pumps for Heating and Cooling*
> Home Agriculture Information Bulletin No. 306
> Agriculture Research Services, U.S.

This bulletin can be purchased from the U.S. Government Printing Office, Washington, D.C. 20402.

Guarantees for air-conditioners and heat pumps. Guarantees for electric central air-conditioners, electric window units and heat pumps differ, depending on the manufacturer. One should expect a five-year guarantee on the compressor, but expensive labor charges are paid by the customer. A one-year guarantee on other parts is customary, with the customer again paying labor costs.

Evaporative coolers. Evaporative coolers are simple cooling devices costing twenty-five to thirty percent less to install than compressor air-conditioners or heat pumps; they are used extensively in dry areas of the United States, such as Arizona, New Mexico, the western part of Texas and southern California. Employing the principle of cooling by evaporation, these coolers make use of wetted media from which water evaporates and cools the air passing through it. Media can be pads made of wood fibers, other fibrous material, or fine screening.

These devices are practical only in arid climates when the dry-bulb temperature is high and the wet-bulb temperature is twenty-five to thirty degrees lower than the dry-bulb temperature. (See Glossary for definition of dry- and wet-bulb temperatures.) In climates where the difference is less, the air contains too much moisture and evaporation will be inhibited so that effective cooling will not take place.

Evaporative coolers have deservedly taken over the nickname *swamp coolers;* the water sometimes contains algae and bacteria which die and give off a characteristic fish smell when the cooler has not been used for a time. The remedies depend on the type and manufacturer. Some systems treat the water; others "bleed" off a certain percentage of the water periodically if the water recirculates, or, if water is plentiful, use fresh water continously.

The media of any type of evaporative cooler will collect mineral deposits and scaling which will cut down efficiency. A prospective buyer of a house should look carefully for this type of deterioration and the attendant fish smell before he makes his decision to accept this economical air-conditioning. The mineral-covered or scaling media are replaceable.

This cooling equipment with its potential difficulties can be used effectively, however, and will produce cooled air having a temperature about five degrees above the wet-bulb temperature. Albuquerque, New Mexico, for example, which has a design summer dry-bulb temperature of roughly ninety-four degrees and a wet-bulb temperature of about sixty-five degrees will produce cooled air at about seventy degrees. Because there is no need of a heavy compressor, the cost of operation is relatively small.

Wetted-pad type. The common wetted-pad type contains evaporative pads usually made of aspen wood fibers, and a water circulating pump; this lifts the water contained in a sump up to a distributing system, from which it runs down the pad and back

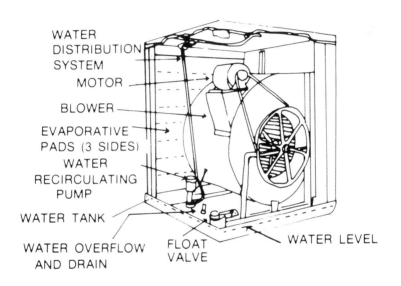

Fig. 36. The wetted-pad evaporative cooler.

Courtesy of American Society of Heating, Refrigerating, and Air-Conditioning Engineers, Inc.

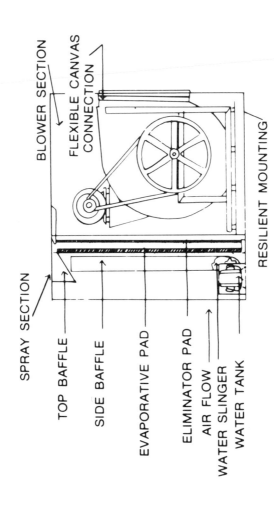

Fig. 37. The slinger evaporative cooler.

Courtesy of American Society of Heating, Refrigerating, and Air-Conditioning Engineers, Inc.

166

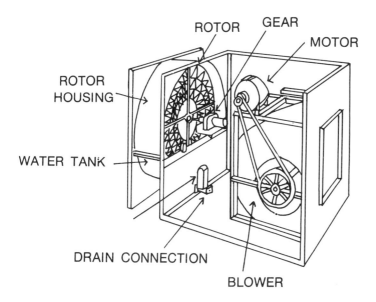

ROTOR GEAR

MOTOR

ROTOR
HOUSING

WATER TANK

DRAIN CONNECTION

BLOWER

Fig. 38. Rotary evaporative cooler.

Courtesy of American Society of Heating, Refrigerating, and Air-Conditioning Engineers, Inc.

into the sump. A blower within the cooler pulls the air through the pads and delivers it by ducts to the space to be cooled. The evaporation pads act as air filters and are effective in removing particles of dust, fine sand, and pollen from the air stream. In some units supplementary filters are used to filter out smaller particles.

Slinger type. The slinger evaporative cooler contains a water slinger to throw a spray of water into the air and onto an evaporation pad commonly made of aspen or glass fiber. Like the wetted-pad type, a blower draws air through the media and delivers it to the house. In areas where sand and dust storms occur, permanent washable intake filters should be provided. It is important that the entire unit be level when installed for proper slinger operation.

167

Rotary type. The rotary type employs a large water wheel containing a meshwork of bronze screening or other types of water-catching material; the lower part of this rotates in a reservoir of water. A blower draws air through the meshwork which contains droplets of waters, and delivers it to the house. Some rotary evaporators feature an adjustable wheel speed; for a dry area the rotating wheel can be made to go faster, and for a wet area slower. The wheel system is similar to the rotating wheel system commonly used in home humidifers, but the similarity ends there.

Capacity of evaporative coolers. Unlike electric compressor or absorption air-conditioners, which are rated in terms of BTU/hr, capacity for a piece of evaporative equipment is given in terms of cubic feet per minute (CFM) of air delivered to a house. This method is understandable when one considers the large dependence and variation of output on climatic conditions where the equipment is installed.

7. SOME CLIMATE CONTROL DEVICES

HUMIDIFIERS

If a humidifier comes with the house, it may be one of the four following principal types:

Plate humidifier. If it's a plate humidifier (see Glossary) connected to the plenum of the furnace, consider it almost worthless. Even when new it will produce very little moisture. Furthermore, it will collect lime deposits on the plates, making them inefficient and their frequent renewal necessary.

Revolving drum and atomizing humidifiers. Two much better types are the revolving drum (or disc) type which picks up water in a reservoir and changes it to tiny droplets, and another which produces humidity by a device that atomizes water. Both are connected to the plenum of the furnace (or a hot-air duct) and introduce water to the stream of air being forced through the ducts by the furnace blower.

Wet-pad humidifier. Another good type which is mounted on the plenum, is the wet-pad type, or one in which water cascades over a pad or a grille like a slow-moving and sparse waterfall.

Lime deposits and need for cleaning humidifiers. All these types are subject to lime deposits and need cleaning, once or twice a year in geographical areas where the water is moderately hard, and quite often in areas where it is very hard. The atomizer-spray type will leave deposits; while the portable atomizing type *for room operation* should be avoided. It is satisfactory for operation in a furnace plenum, because the deposits form harmlessly on the inside of the ducts.

Methods of mounting. Any plenum-mounted humidifier should not be mounted on the side of a return duct to the furnace; this will seriously impair efficiency. The hot air in the furnace plenum will accept more moisture than the colder air in the return duct.

More and more units are appearing on the market that channel air from the return duct through the humidifier; the air then continues through the plenum, bypassing the furnace. This method of mounting is not highly efficient.

Testing for proper operation. Operation of the humidifier should be checked by temporarily raising the setting of the humidistat to a high humidity value. This will make the humidifier operate regardless of the humidity in the house. Once the setting has been made and the water supply checked for operation, and after a minute delay from the time the furnace blower begins operating, the humidifier should start working. (This check may not be possible in the summer because the high humidity may keep the humidistat satisfied so it won't activate the humidifier.) Next, if the humidity-making device is of the revolving drum, disc, or wet-pad type, turn off the electric switch controlling furnace operation, and take off the apparatus cover for a detailed inspection. Then, turn the furnace switch back on and check for proper movement of the working parts: the drum or disc should turn slowly and smoothly through the water in the reservoir, or water should cascade over the wet pad, and in all cases the little fan that blows tiny particles of water into the air stream should operate. Finally, make sure there is sufficient water in the reservoir to nearly fill it. (WARNING: Be extremely wary of electrical wiring underneath which can be exposed in some humidifiers.)

Capacity of Humidifiers. It is difficult to determine humidifier capacity required, i.e., the required water furnished by the device to a house in one day. Many factors are involved: among these are the amount of moisture generated in a house by cooking, showers, washing, clothes drying, size of house, the number of cracks which allow the outdoor air to enter the house, and the dryness of the air in your geographical area. Some humidifiers on the market make no claim to capacity; others do.

Be sure that the humidifier installed on the furnace generates at least fifteen gallons a day, especially if the house has three bedrooms and there are a lot of kids to cause considerable cooking and washing. Some small, tightly sealed houses, however, with the same number of children, may need no humidifier. Houses larger than three-bedroom houses probably need more than fifteen gallons.

It is possible for a humidifier to have too much capacity, particularly in the cold climates that occur in states or areas like Montana, Wisconsin and northern New York. Too much humidity can cause heavy frosting on windows on exceedingly cold days — which can cause water damage to the woodwork. The humidistat which controls operation can be adjusted during the extremely cold and dry days to prevent frost or window fogging. Don't be alarmed if a moderate amount of frost forms on the panes of storm windows of the coldest rooms in the house.

DEHUMIDIFIERS

Dehumidifiers take the moisture out of the air during the summer months, and are particularly useful for inhibiting the growth of mildew and keeping basements dry. They are usually portable.

An air-conditioning system in the part of the house that needs dehumidifying automatically takes moisture out of the air, in which case a dehumidifier may not be needed. In many geographical areas south of Pennsylvania, it is not unusual to see humidifiers used in rooms even with air-conditioning, particularly when the basement area is deep in the ground.

The type that drains off water accumulated from the air by a pipe or hose to a floor-drain is best. Another satisfactory type is one that shuts off automatically when the drain pan has filled up.

The dehumidifier is really an air-conditioner that delivers no net cooling because the evaporator which cools, and the condenser which heats, are in the same room. Frosting on the honeycomb-like fins of the evaporator coils is an indication of a leak in the refrigerant line and an early demise of the equipment.

ELECTRONIC AIR FILTERS

An electronic air filter installed in the return duct of a furnace or indoor unit of an air-conditioner (or heat pump), can be a real bonus. It is an expensive piece of equipment and, if working properly, adds to the quality of the air-filtering in a home.

All particles coming into this filter are charged electrically. When they travel with the air downstream on the way to the furnace or air-conditioner, they are attracted to metal plates charged with electricity of opposite polarity. In the less expensive models, they remain on the plates until they are cleaned off manually. In the more expensive models the plates are cleaned automatically. The high voltage necessary to charge the particles and plates is generated in an electric assembly known as the power pack.

Since the electronic filter does not catch lint efficiently, a fibrous pre-filter is often placed in the air stream ahead of it. This pre-filter helps to prolong the period between cleanings. It looks similar to the ordinary furnace air filter but is more efficient.

Efficiency of electronic air filters. The increase in efficiency over the drug-store type of glass-fiber filter is great. It collects nearly 100 percent of the finer dust particles and smoke particles that come into the air current, and a reasonable amount of pollen and spores which find their way into the house and get to the filter. If it has a pre-filter, the overall catching ability is even higher.

172

All these features help keep the furnace or air-conditioner in good working condition by protecting the working parts or coils from dust or lint which could seriously impair efficiency. The electronic filter could also be helpful to members of the house who are allergic to pollen and dust.

One must realize, though, that this high efficiency does not mean that the house you purchase will be entirely free of dust, smoke or lint. Only a portion of the air in the house travels in the air-circuit of the furnace of air-conditioner and through the filter. The rest either settles on the furnishings, floor, and windowsills, or gets sucked into the vacuum cleaner. Much of it gets stirred around in the air and falls back to the floor.

Disadvantages of electronic air filters. This type of filter, with its good qualities, does have some disadvantages: (1) the problem of cleaning off deposits, and (2) the possibility of generation of ozone if the applied voltage becomes too high. At a high level

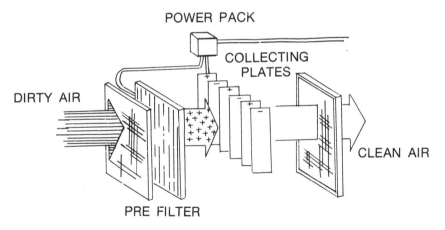

Fig. 39. The electronic air filter cleans when electronically-charged particulate matter (dust, pollen, etc.) is attracted to electronically-charged plates, bearing opposite polarity.

Courtesy of National Environmental Systems Contractors Association.

this active gas can be dangerous to breathe. Because it has a characteristically pungent smell that occurs during rainstorms when lightning has struck nearby, one can usually detect it.

High voltage and the resultant ozone can occur where a previous owner had failed to clean the plates and jacked up the voltage to compensate for loss of efficiency. However, you as an operator can have a safe and efficient piece of equipment if you follow the manufacturer's instructions carefully. The filter also does restrict the air flow somewhat, a not too serious disadvantage if the plates and prefilter are kept reasonably clean. There are mechanical filters that use fibrous media that causes more restriction than this type of filter.

VENTILATING FANS

A large ventilating fan which uses much less energy than an air conditioner is always an asset during the summer. It may be installed in the attic next to one of the end louvers, in a window, near an exhaust grille in a porch roof, or in a soffit. On occasion it may be placed in a wall. It may pull the air from the entire house or it may just ventilate the attic.

Attic ventilation

When installed and confined to pulling air across the attic, the fan is effective because it removes large amounts of hot air and reduces the heatflow downward. If the attic, however, has six inches of glass fiber insulation or more between the joists, the net effectiveness is not great.

If this attic fan has sufficient capacity, it will help bring comfort and will reduce the energy and cost of air-conditioning as well. It should have sufficient capacity to produce one-half to one air change in the attic per minute, or *at least* three cubic feet per minute (CFM) for each square foot of floor area; e.g., required capacity equals three times the number of square feet on the attic floor. This figure-of-merit should be greater in southern states and less in northern states. The fan should be discharging in the same direction as the flow of the prevailing winds.

Many fans will show their capacity on the nameplate, which depends, among other things, on fan speed, blade length, blade angle and shape of blade. A number of combinations is possible, but the general rule is that a large fan with a small horsepower motor is better from the point of view of noise, than a small fan with a larger motor. A twenty-four inch blade (diameter measurement) with a 1/4 horsepower motor is usually needed for a medium size attic (5000 cu. ft.) in a moderately warm geographical area. A two or three speed model is recommended.

Most fans are rated on a free-air delivery basis; this means that the specified CFM will be obtained if there are no obstructions to air movement. But in a real situation there are louvers and screens at the fan exhaust; as a consequence there will be twenty-five percent less air-delivery than that specified.

Attic fans can be hooked up to work with a thermostat as well as with a manual switch controlled from downstairs. This thermostat control offers a real convenience of operation during the

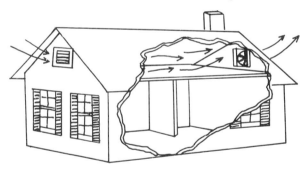

Fig. 40. Ventilation pattern for attic ventilation.

Courtesy of Lau Industries.

hot summer season. Fan operation in winter is an asset for reducing build-up of moisture and condensation in the attic.

Ventilation of entire house with attic fan. Often house occupants will use an exhaust attic fan to cool the entire house;

in this case the door to the attic stairway must be left open, or ceilinglouvers must be employed. A window (or windows) should be opened in the living quarters below to allow outdoor air to enter. This operation requires a fan with more CFM capacity than the type used just for attic cooling. Size, of course, depends on how large the whole house is, in terms of total room volume. Check this volume, excluding rooms and closets where no cooling is desired. For one air-change per minute, the CFM should be numerically equal to the volume of the house. Geographical areas south of the middle states will require a larger fan and those north, a smaller fan. A thirty inch fan is normally the minimum size considered.

A fan designed for an attic can be installed in a window in an upper hallway. It is useful in cooling the entire house. Make calculations the same way.

The greatest benefit from the fan during hot summer weather will come after 6 p.m. when the outdoor temperature begins to slide down, and when the occupants are asleep. One which can be adjusted to a lower and quieter speed when the night air is coolest, is best. Don't forget to check the operation of the fan, if manually-controlled, when you walk through the house; listen for noise and excessive vibration.

Ventilating entire house with window fans. Window fans typically have a capacity of about 2000 CFM and have a twenty inch fan blade. Most have a high speed and a low speed, but some have three speeds. It is best if the fan can be easily removed from its mount so it can be put away in the winter and the lower window-pane closed.

A good twenty inch fan can change the air in a twenty by fifteen by eight foot room about once a minute. Some fans feature reverse operations so it can serve to exhaust the room air or bring cool air in; this is advantageous. Check operation when you are near windows.

See the July 1974 issue of Consumer Reports for additional information on attic fans.

8. SECURING YOUR HOUSE AGAINST BURGLARY

LOCKS

The primary defense against intruders in a house is the locking mechanisms on the doors. Look at them, try them, and evaluate carefully. Two types of locks — the key-in-the-knob type and the mortise type — are used more than any other on doors.

The key-in-the-knob lock. The least safe is the key-in-the-knob type; it is found in most new houses, and in a few cases can be readily opened by an intruder who slips a celluloid card between the door jamb and the beveled latch, pushing the latch inward to remove it from its keeper in the door jamb. Better key-in-the-knob locks have a trigger bolt, consisting of a small half-round cylinder next to the beveled latch, to prevent this from happening. A typical lock of this type, with or without the trigger bolt, has a locking button on the inside knob. This, when turned or set, serves to lock and unlock the door from the inside.

There are other methods for preventing the intruder from slipping the card in. One method is to provide an offset to cover the crack between the door and the door jamb. Another is to replace the old, flat lock plate that lies flush to the door jamb with a lock plate that has an extension of metal, the same thickness as the plate, that extends out at an angle and covers this crack.

In cases where the door of the house has the key-in-the-knob type and you want more security than the trigger bolt or crack-covering techniques provide, plan on installing another kind of

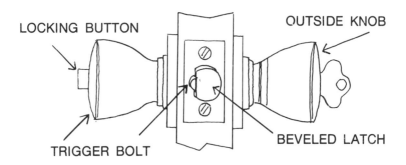

LOCKING BUTTON
OUTSIDE KNOB
TRIGGER BOLT
BEVELED LATCH

Fig. 41. Key-in-the-knob lock.

Courtesy of Consumers Union.

lock. However, changing to a stronger and safer lock is time-consuming because better locks usually require a larger diameter hole in the door.

Mortise lock. The safer mortise lock has a dead bolt and a convenience latch, both of which lock the door. The dead bolt, a non-beveled, square-edged, sturdy, and tongue-like device, goes in and out of the hole in the lock plate and door jamb. It is turned either by a key in a lock on the outside, or by thumb-turn on the inside of the door. The knobs, inside and out, operate the beveled convenience latch much the same as they do in the key-in-the-knob lock. This latch, unprotected by a trigger bolt, can in many cases be moved inward by the intruder's card, but it makes no difference because the dead bolt is fastened in the separate lock. This convenience latch can be locked by pushing one of the two latch buttons which are mounted in the lock and flush to the door edge. (CAUTION: the door must be bolted for safety and dependence must not be placed on locking by the latch button.)

For the mortise type it is important that the dead bolt is long. Poor locks provide a dead bolt as short as 1/2 inch. Better locks provide a bolt of one full inch. While the mortise lock may provide more security than the key-in-the-knob type, it too can be defeated; an auxiliary lock may be desirable.

Auxiliary locks. The vertical-bolt auxiliary lock is one of the

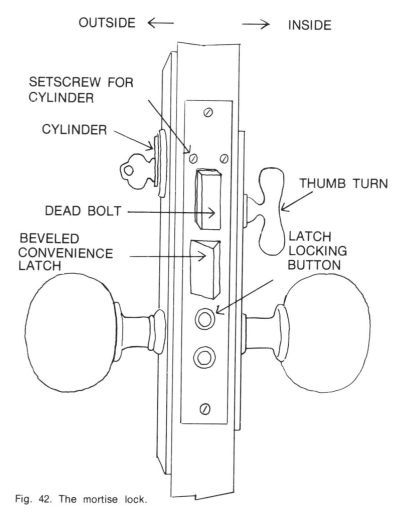

OUTSIDE ⟵   ⟶ INSIDE

SETSCREW FOR
CYLINDER

CYLINDER

THUMB TURN

DEAD BOLT

BEVELED
CONVENIENCE
LATCH

LATCH
LOCKING
BUTTON

Fig. 42. The mortise lock.

Courtesy of Consumers Union.

best and is almost completely jimmy-proof. When mounted on the inside of the door, it is secured to its mating plate on the door jamb just as a hinge is secured to its mating plate: two bolts go down through two cylindrical holes. The bolt is activated on the inside by a thumb turn and on the outside by a key.

Do not count on a chain guard: a good pair of snips can cut through the chain. Once the door is partially open, ramming from the outside can usually rip a chain device from its mooring. A special purpose device such as an electronic lock alarm that emits a piercing noise when tampered with, will be helpful if it comes with the house, but a vertical-bolt auxiliary lock probably offers more security since it does more to preclude entry. Some intruders may not be dissuaded by the alarm.

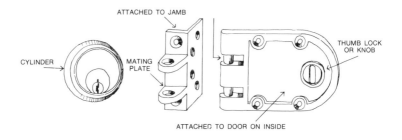

Fig. 43. Vertical-bolt auxiliary lock.

Courtesy of Consumers Union.

Double-key locks. None of the auxiliary locks previously mentioned will hold if the glass or panel is broken by an intruder since he can merely reach in and turn the thumb knob. In this case, protection can be offered only by a double-keyed lock that requires a key to lock and unlock the door from the outside as well as from the inside. A similar arrangement can be installed on windows which require a single key, so an intruder cannot break the glass and reach in and open the window lock; complete window destruction is required before he can enter.

180

Other security precautions. The house you are inspecting may have bars or a strong metal mesh grillwork on the first floor windows and doors. These protective devices will be helpful in high crime areas. The bars or grillwork should be secured to the window and door framework by strong bolts or other secure means to be effective.

An alarm system is also valuable in high-crime areas. However, these alarm systems can be trigger-happy and generate nerve-jamming false alarms.

Security measures go well beyond bars, locks and alarms. Others which can help are:

- Storm windows.
- Good exterior house lighting.
- Spot lights controllable from the bedroom.
- Street lights and general area lighting.
- Fences.
- Peep hole in door.
- High first-floor windows.
- Door speaker, usually connected with an inter-communication set.
- Garage doors that may be opened from the car with a radio signal.

For more detailed information on locks and security measures read the February 1971 issue of Consumer Reports.

9. SPECIAL TYPES OF HOUSES
AND THEIR SPECIAL PROBLEMS

THE COUNTRY HOUSE

The well. Many of the problems suffered by country house owners center around the well. If the well is new, information about it is usually available from the county, town, or township. Ask questions of the present owner and contact the local pump and well digger for service records. Find the answers to these questions.

- How pure is the water? The county Environmental Health officer will test a sample of the water for possible contamination. He is interested in the coliform count, as an indication of surface contamination.
- What is the rate of water flow? How much water can be pumped out of the well with constant use before it starts churning mud and is dry? A well that produces less than four gallons per minute precludes watering the lawn. Set this figure as a minimum supply unless you are willing to provide some special storage apparatus.
- How deep is the well? The old wells, dug about twenty to thirty feet deep, are no longer satisfactory and in most cases not approved. The best wells are drilled wells. They are usually encased with six inch pipe through the dirt layers and into rock. Depth will vary in different areas, but is usually about 100 feet. In some of the shore areas, it not uncommon to drill for 200 to 500 feet to reach pure water.

Water is pumped out with either a jet pump which is placed next to a storage pressure tank in the basement or well house, or a submersible pump that actually fits down into the wall casing. Both are satisfactory.

One of the most obvious questions often overlooked is that of location. Sooner or later the well will need servicing and you should record its location in advance. The well should be uphill from both the house and septic system, and 100 feet from the leaching area.

Your test of the well should include a visual examination of the pump motor and pressure storage tank. Run water simultaneously from several spigots for about fifteen minutes and note the pressure fluctuations. Near the end of the test look for mud and cloudiness in the water, an indication the water is being drawn off faster than it is being supplied.

This test is also good to help you determine if there is back-up stoppage from the septic tank. Remember that a power failure will mean no water; if the house is in an area where there are frequent electrical storms and power failures, a portable generator is convenient.

Sewage disposal. Sewage disposal on individual lots is now done with a combination of septic tanks and leaching areas. Raw sewage, the household waste, goes through drain pipes and into a water tight concrete tank that should have a capacity of at least 1,000 gallons. There the solid matter is broken down by an anaerobic bacterial action. The discharge, a rather clear effluent, flows from the tank into a leaching area. This leaching area may be a large gravel bed slightly below the surface, trenches with drain tile, or, deep cylindrical pits constructed of cinder block.

If the soil is suitable for absorption (percolation), there will be no evidence of sewage water working to the surface. Obtain whatever information you can about soil conditions from the local environmental health department and the owner. The local septic tank cleaning service will be able to provide some information. A neighbor on the down-wind side of a malfunc-

184

tioning system will also be eager to volunteer all he knows. These are the questions you will need to ask:

- Where is the tank and leaching area? (They should be downhill from the house and well, and accessible by truck.)
- What type of system is it, and what is its capacity?
- When was it installed and, most important, has it been altered, improved or enlarged? If so, why?
- What is the rate of percolation? Ask the county Health Department for figures. Is it good percolation or is it poor? Poor percolation usually means continuous trouble.
- What is the service record of tank pumping? Once a year is too often but, on the other hand, if it was never pumped the tank is surely filled with solids; it will clog the leaching area and destroy the system, which is not recoverable. A pumping/cleaning record of every three to six years is considered a normal preventative maintenance schedule. By design all systems are eventually doomed to failure, but with regular tank cleaning, a system will last twenty to thirty years.
- Is there recovery room on your lot? Usually this is no problem on an acre or more, but half-acre lots can be trouble if they are surrounded by an area of other half acre sites. There may be no room to place a new system and the soil will become saturated.

To check the functioning of the septic system, run the water and watch the lowest plumbing fixture in the house for back-up. Outside, look for rich green thick grass in the area of the leaching system. It may look lush but indicates poor absorption and during wet spells may stink. The fluids working to the surface may produce harmful bacteria and contaminate a neighbor's well. When there is snow on the ground, a bare spot (from heat) may help you to locate the tank and leaching area.

If you are planning to remodel or enlarge a house, you may also need to enlarge the sewage system. The county may have record of the original plot of your house and the septic system. This will help you to budget the expense. You may not be completely satisfied with the conditions and details of your septic system, so it is important to know the availability of municipal

185

hook-up. Is it in the street or in the next subdivision? Are you allowed to hook into the system? The cost of maintaining your own sewer and water facilities in most cases exceeds the cost of local tax levy where such facilities are publicly supplied.

The following small pamphlets containing information, diagrams and explanations about septic systems are available through the U. S. Government Printing Office, Washington, D.C. 20402, at a nominal cost.

- Manual of Septic-Tank Practice. (Public Health Service Publication No. 526.)
- A Study of Methods of Preventing Failure of Septic Tank Percolation Systems. (U.S. Department of Housing and Urban Development Publication.)

Public utilities. The energy fuel sources that you have become accustomed to in the city may not be available in the country. These often include piped-in gas or electricity, in which case bottled gas service is used and delivered by local L.P. (liquid propane) distributors. The range and minor appliances are fueled by L.P. The price is usually not competitive with electricity, and is considerably higher than oil or natural gas when used in quantities for central heating.

Other considerations. Beautiful country homes have much acreage which results in a great deal of upkeep. Expansive lawns are great for country gentlemen with paid help, but for busy suburbanites they may be a problem.

Think twice before buying a house which has no trees around it. It will place a large load on the heating systems and the air-conditioner. However, in a newly developed tract in the country you may have no choice.

Proper orientation of the house, especially in northern areas, is especially important. It can provide more sunlight and warmth in winter, less condensation of water on windows, and cooler temperatures in the summer. See Chapter 1.

It is best that the entrance doors be on a side not facing the prevailing winds. Information about these winds can be obtained from the National Weather Service in your area (National Oceanic & Atmospheric Administration, Department of Commerce).

PREFABRICATED HOUSES

Prefabricated houses have been around for a long time. Even before World War II, prefab-kit houses were advertised in popular magazines, and shipped in the form of pre-cut lumber, doors, windows, electric boxes and other house-components, and assembled by handy do-it-yourselfers and family on their own piece of property. Assembly of the parts often took two or three years.

Panelized construction. The next development in prefabricated houses was the panelized, or sectionalized, house, which was shipped from the manufacturer together with kit material in large flat sections — such as walls, roof decks, and floors. Assembly of these houses required the combined effort of a group of carpenters and laborers, but they had the advantage of shorter assembly time. Indeed, because of its efficient construction methods, the panelized house is more popular than all other kinds of prefabrication combined.

Modular house construction. In the late 1960's modular houses arrived — sophisticated in design, constructed at the factory in volumetric sections, and with many of the modern amenities. Assembly of these houses was even quicker; it is common today for one to be put together in a week by a team of experts trained especially for the work.

At first the modular house was considered second-rate and only purchased by do-it-yourselfers low on the economic scale. Now this manufactured house has made its bid to take its place alongside the medium and higher priced conventional, "stick built" house. Some builders predict that it may gradually take the lead.

The modular house is usually shipped to the building site in sections consisting of a half, third, quarter or even a fifth of a house. It doesn't come, as one would expect, in room sections. When manufactured by a reputable company, each section is subjected to rigid quality-control — an advantage the modular manufacturers claim the conventional houses do not have.

Many styles are available, ranging from a small rambler to a large split-level or contemporary. Some are built over attractive masonry foundations. They may have basements, concrete slabs, or crawl spaces. The house is sold by a builder-dealer, who has a clearly defined territory assigned to him by a manufacturer; it is usually assembled by construction experts out of his office.

Certain other items should be inspected carefully by the prospective buyer. It is possible, due to rough treatment during shipment, for nails to come loose and "nail popping" to occur in dry wall panels, or for wooden frame members to be fastened insecurely. Electric wiring is sometimes loose and dangerous to an occupant.

If the joists below a second floor are made of 2 x 8's, instead of 2 x 10's, and/or spacing between them is greater than sixteen in O.C., the floor will show spring; jump up and down on this floor to test. The best two floor houses will have two extra second-floor joists side-by-side around the periphery, with 1/2 inch thick steel sheeting sandwiched between them.

Look carefully at the external siding; plywood siding which shows delamination from weathering may be a negative mark against a house. Make sure that there is sheathing beneath any type of plywood siding. Look carefully at alignment of house on its foundation.

Nearly all modular houses use plastic piping in their drain and waste systems. Inspect the piping at connections. (See Chapter 6.)

In areas where snow load is a problem, look for a roof having a pitch of at least forty-five degrees, especially in the older pre-modular prefab houses where truss construction was not used. Low slope roofs are easier to handle in transit by the modular manufacturer. They must be trussed in areas with heavy snow.

The prefab house employs many of the latest construction

features. A good house will use truss construction in the attic, double-glazed windows, seamless aluminum gutters, siding of aluminum or composition material, proper insulation in the attic, floor, and wall, and wall-to-wall carpeting. Air conditioning is often included.

Because of the production line methods and requirements for assembly at the site, many innovative features are employed. For example, the internal piping and electrical wiring is enclosed in a package known as a utility core; this is a one foot wide hollow rectangular section between the kitchen and another room in the house.

When you look at a modular house, investigate the reputation of the manufacturer and builder-dealer before you commit yourself. Many mobile-home manufacturers, and other manufacturers unfamiliar with special modular construction techniques, are moving into the field.

A significant disadvantage of modular housing is the uniformity of design. Therefore it may be important to you to determine if houses of the design you are considering are to be erected later in the neighborhood.

Regardless of the type of prefab house, many of the suggestions and admonitions made in earlier chapters for conventional houses apply. Look for gaps between the foundation wall and the adjoining framing. Look for windows that do not open easily, or doors that do not close entirely. On a cold windy day, you may notice an exceptionally strong draft when you place your hand near a wall switch or receptacle. Consider such a thing when you make your offer of a price. Look for and ask about proper insulation.

Codes regulating prefab houses. Local code-enforcing agencies have until recently been in a quandary on how to inspect concealed elements behind the pre-panelized or prefabricated enclosures. The code-enforcers have been unjustly accused of conservatism retarding production-line benefits, but in good civic spirit they have been protecting people in their jurisdictions against hidden defects.

Just recently several states have set up a system of trained personnel and certifying bodies to control quality in and out of their state. As an example of such control, in the State of Maryland no mobile home or prefabricated unit can be certified for occupancy unless it complies with B.O.A.C. codes. (B.O.A.C. is a national organization of building-code authorities.) These homes are inspected at various stages of completion at the factory. Should your state have such a system you will be protected against concealed defects.

MOBILE HOMES

The mobile home is an outgrowth of the old house trailer, and so far is the only real low-cost housing. These homes have such problems as fire hazards and inadequate anchoring to protect them from high winds. They have nonetheless gained a significant portion of the housing market.

10. REMODELLING AND RENOVATING SECOND-HAND HOUSES

It is often advantageous, because of relative price or because of short commuting distance, to buy a turn-of-the-century or even older house and renovate it. Often this is fun — the project gives the buyer a chance to get some exercise and to vent some ideas of his or her own, and it is often profitable as well.

Newer second-hand houses, those no more than forty years old, may be a good buy despite first impressions. Often such houses are technically sound, and only cosmetic improvements are necessary. Sometimes removing things, such as heavy porches, gingerbread, or overgrown trees, up-dates the appearance of a house more than expensive add-ons.

RENOVATING VERY OLD HOUSES

There are pitfalls, however, which a prospective buyer should weigh carefully before he purchases a forty to seventy-five year old house. Hidden behind the walls may be completely worn-out galvanized piping or dangerous and tangled electric wiring; the lathing behind the plaster may need replacing after this renovation work is done. You may have to soup up the amperage supply, possibly inserting new wiring, a new electric panel, and a new service entrance cable. The new service cable will probably be made of aluminum, which could pose a problem with panel boxes originally designed for copper wire.

Danger from leaded paint. The greatest pitfall of all is the danger that comes from sanding and scraping leaded paint in old houses. If the house was built before 1940, it is likely that lethal lead was used as part of the pigment in the paint, either on the interior or exterior. In houses built between 1940 and 1955, the danger decreased. Voluntary safety standards were set up in 1955. Houses built after that time seldom contained lead paint.

It is important that a mask be worn indoors for scraping and sanding painted surfaces. The scrapings should be placed in a tight container for disposal. The container should be kept out of reach of children between the ages of one and eight, who may eat it, and should be disposed of in accordance with local health regulations. Your local field inspection office will be glad to give you advice on this matter. Even if the scraping is done outdoors, be careful and avoid dust; a mask wouldn't hurt.

Lack of insulation. Very old houses are completely uninsulated; often the brick or stonework has direct contact with the plaster on the interior walls. Not only does an avalanche of heat pass through the walls to the outside, but often water seeps into the indoors. This water leakage can be compounded by a leaking gutter above the wall. To repair the leaking, replace mortar voids in the masonry and pour roof coating into the gutter. You may need to replace the gutter.

For insulation you can build a false dry wall or wood panel wall furred out from the original plaster. The new wall must be furred out with wood furring strips. Circumstances dictate the width of these furring strips and the amount of space between the panels and the plaster wall. Often, due to the dimensions of the wood framing around windows and doors, the false wall can only be furred out so there is a 3/4 inch space between the panels and the wall: furring strips of this thickness are readily available.

With this limitation it is practicable to use drywall with a reflective aluminum backing, so the air space plus the reflective backing will offer moderate insulation. If you prefer wood panels, you can get the same effect by nailing reflective insulation directly to the furring strips and then nailing the panels over the shiny material.

It is also possible to create a wider space using two by two inch furring strips. It is advisable here to place fiberglass or other mineral wool blanket material behind the panels. The material should be about one and one-half inch thick (R-5). As in the case of the 3/4 inch space, drywall panels with reflective insulation (or separate reflective insulation behind wood panels) can be used.

Finally, you can furr out using two inch by four inch studs which are actually three and one-half inches thick. Place three and one-half inch fiberglass (R-11) and reflective insulation behind the panels. Never allow the fiberglass material to touch the old plaster, which may be damp. Keep the reflective insulation on the warm side of the fibrous insulation. It is possible to use balsa wood, which has good insulation properties, instead of fiberglass.

You may use foamed plastic behind the panels, but avoid using it behind wood panels which have an unfavorable fire endurance rating — even though it has been treated to inhibit combustion and fire spread. Use 5/8 inch type X improved drywall panels which have a good fire endurance rating. During construction, never leave the foamed material exposed because of danger of fire.

Additional safeguard against moisture from the outside is to place a sheet of plastic polyvinyl chloride or polyethylene against the plaster and behind the false wall. Use short hardened nails. Glue or mastic will not work.

RENOVATING NEWER SECOND-HAND HOUSES

Renovating a newer second-hand house (i.e., one no more than forty years old) can also have problems. Some roof leaks are difficult to find, some leaky basements stubbornly keep on leaking no matter what you do, etc. Be wary and make stubborn but judicious inquiries before you buy. Code requirements can present difficulties; for example, a new, heavier-capacity water heater may require a larger hole in the chimney to accommodate a larger flue pipe, or a window may be blocked reducing required ventilation. Many of the pointers presented in the preceding pages for a very old house apply for a newer second-hand house.

Peeling paint on brick houses. Sometimes a homeowner will repaint a house two or three times and it still blisters. This may be avoided by using correct techniques.

An oil-based paint may be used over a chalky surface after brushing the chalk away with a wire brush. Latex paint may be used but *very careful surface conditioning,* involving scraping and water-washing, is required. When using an oil-base paint, it is very important that the surface be completely dry. This is also preferable, although not required, for a latex coating.

There are other reasons for paint failure on brick walls. One is dampness coming from inside the house. Sometimes moisture migrates because the humidity inside is excessive (a maximum of fifty percent relative humidity at sixty-eight degrees indoor temperature is a good rate to follow). At other times, the moisture might migrate from the ground, or the walls may remain wet from rainfall. Under these circumstances in warm, damp climates, mildew might result; to cure mildew dilute a common household bleach such as *Clorox.* Scrub with a brush, and wash well with clean water following treatment.

An uncommon cause of paint failure is efflorescence, which is a deposit of salts on the brickwork. It is evidenced by a whitish bloom or encrustation. The deposit must be removed before repainting is attempted. If the house is reasonably old (eight to twenty), wash with a detergent and rinse off thoroughly with water. If the house is newer, wash with an acid solution of muriatic acid — a commercial name for hydrochloric acid. An acid concentration of five percent volume is common but concentrates as high as twenty percent are used. Following the acid application, neutralize thoroughly with water.

Scraping and painting. Repainting the walls and wood trim of a room is usually simple. However, repainting of the ceiling can require considerable work or expense, if contracted out.

Scrape and sand the old drywall or plaster wall if it is cracked, flaked, or peeling. Paint patches that cannot be scraped off can remain. Next, paint with a primer-sealer. The purpose of the sealer is to prevent the first coat from being sucked into the surface, thus requiring an additional finish coat. Use the appropriate sealer for the type of paint you intend to use; e.g., a primer sealer manufactured for use with latex paint, or one designed especially for oil-base paint. (Don't let a paint salesperson sell you a primer; you need a *primer sealer.*)

The finish coat can be one of a number of types. The three common types are latex, oil-base and polyvinyl acetate (PVA); the latter is sometimes a latex paint. If you use latex paint or PVA, be sure there is no chalk on the surface. If you use oil-base paint, be sure that the surface is dry. Finally, apply the finish coat with either a brush or roller.

If you replace some of the old trim with new wood, apply a primer coat to seal the wood, so the paint for the finish coat will not sink in and leave a splotchy finish. You can use enamel, semi-gloss or flat (matte) paint for the finish. If the wood trim is old, paint the finish coat without bothering about the primer.

For painting the ceiling, a special treatment may be necessary. In the process of scraping and sanding, thick patches of the old paint may remain. Some of the plaster or drywall may fall out when the peeling paint is removed, resulting in an uneven surface. To repair this unevenness and to develop an even texture, apply spackle in the worst depressions. A skim coat of plaster-topping mix applied over the repaired surface will make it smooth and even. Topping mixes, such as that manufactured by the U. S. Gypsum Co., or a mix having the Gold Bond trade name, are commonly available. A binding agent should be used over the old plaster to provide adhesion for the new skim coat; this is especially important if there was serious trouble with the old paint flaking off. Following these applications, paint with a sealer-primer, then with as many finish coats as necessary. Use professional help, if the condition of the ceiling is too bad.

Air pollution may also pose a problem to the painter; discoloration may appear on large areas of the surface, or in spots, and must be properly cleaned. The problem is complicated; the cause and solution depends on the products manufactured in local factories. The Air Pollution Control Association, 4400 Fifth Avenue, Pittsburgh, Pennsylvania, 15213, may be able to give some help if you can tell them the nature of the effluent factory products.

Blown insulation. One of the most frustrating and puzzling problems is to know what to do with a house about thirty or forty years old that has no insulation in the walls. Insulating companies are available who will blow loose insulation into these walls through a large hose; it helps, but doesn't serve as well as new insulation. It may be blown in from the top and might be stopped by a horizontal structural member, or some other obstruction, and will not completely fill the void behind the wall; even if it does, the loose fill will settle through the years. You may elect to build up a furred dry-wall or wood paneling against the old cold inside plaster wall.

Peeling gutters and downspouts. A common paint failure in an old house occurs on the gutters and downspouts. Sometimes it is better simply to replace them with new ones. Before you make the decision, consider the work — and even danger involved — in cleaning and repainting the old gutters. The four following procedures are absolutely necessary.

First, clean them with a paint cleaner, a gelatinous type of material with a methylene chloride base. (Be careful not to breathe the fumes or let the methylene chloride get in to your eyes.) Brush this material on a gutter surface about three feet long, allowing it to react with the paint for about twenty minutes. Then scrape off the cleaner, and the coating of paint that has shriveled up up with the treatment, with a wire brush. In some instances, the paint will stick and must be removed with a knife; when a few small patches will not come off at all, just leave them. While scraping, another three foot length can be undergoing chemical reaction.

Second, wash off the remains of the paint cleaner with turpentine solvent, making sure that the solvent in the wiping rag is always clean.

Third, apply a good primer. The best primer contains zinc dust, but a primer with a zinc-oxide base will do. (NOTE: Some contain leaded pigments and are so advertised on the can.)

Finally, after the primer has dried for a full day, apply two coats of oil-base or latex paint. Be sure the gutters are dry if oil-base paint is used.

If you decide to replace the gutters, you may use the light-weight and pre-painted seamless aluminum type. The average aluminum gutter is unable to withstand the battering from ladders during leaf-cleaning time as well as a steel gutter does; a more expensive type that will stand the punishment of the ladder.

Leaky basements. There are a few cardinal rules to be followed when repairing leaky basements. The ground next to a house should slope away from it. Gutters should not leak, and the water from the downspouts should be carried away a safe distance by a drain pipe or splash pan. Most leaky basements can be traced to poor drainage.

Second, be careful about contracting with a company which promises to stop the leaks by pumping a clay-like material known as bentonite into the dirt close to the basement wall. The Council of Better Business Bureaus advises, that the procedure "without additional work should be considered appropriate only when the soil is not hard-packed and the water table is lower than any part of the basement." Furthermore, the procedure may run into hundreds of dollars. It is difficult to determine if the company submitting the proposal is willing to make an accurate and honest analysis of soil conditions, and probability of success, before the work begins.

Third, the best but most expensive way to stop leaks is to patch on the outside. Pressure of water and wet soil from the outside will force small particles into the wall where the patching is not perfectly done. A french drain around the outside of the foundation wall is the only solution (see Glossary).

Because of the expense involved in sealing the outside wall or building a french drain, many homeowners resort to patching or painting the inside of the wall. Basement walls with small leaks might be effectively waterproofed by plastering them with two 3/8 inch thick coats of Portland cement mortar. When the leakage is small and occurs only during a short period of the year, the walls may be treated with two or three brush-applied coats of Portland cement grout (a grout consists of a mixture of cement, water and sand, having the consistency of thick cream). Cement water paints, which are sold under various trade names in the stores, will reduce the rate of leakage, but are less effective than the mortar or grout coats.

Finally, if a house is situated in a neighborhood where the water table is abnormally high, the homeowner must resort to the use of a drainage system under the basement floor and a sump pump that automatically and periodically pumps water out of a water hole (sump). Before you decide on the house, visit the neighbors to find out more about area water problems.

Repair of stucco. A large patch of stucco may be applied by trowelling on a prepared cement mix. The first step is replacing the steel lath underneath with a new lath or a piece of chicken wire. Next, rough up the wet cement with a pronged instrument or stick to prepare it to receive the second and final smooth coat. If an exposed aggregate-finish is desired, throw a scattering of pea-size gravel into the wet material.

Usually this patch will not match the old stucco and the entire stucco surface on the house should be repainted. Be sure that the cement is completely dry before repainting the patch, particularly if oil-base paint is used.

To repair cracks in stucco, apply patching "cement" with a caulking gun. Cut off the pointed, plastic end of the cement tube so the cement issuing from it matches the thickness of the crack under repair.

Addition of a new room. An additional room, if well constructed and provided with ample heating and cooling, will add to the resale value of the house. If you are interested in adding a room, first consider local code requirements. Space is the prime consideration; for example, you can't build too close to the next house.

It is not always wise for you to build this addition yourself. Many costly mistakes are possible, especially in electrical and plumbing work. On the other hand, check the reputation of any builder before you sign a contract.

If you do decide to build yourself, go to a reputable lumber yard, place your problem before a clerk and stick with him through the entire process. He will help you not only with the lumber problems, but will give you good advice about concrete foundations, picture windows, wall framing, and other structural components. Usually he will be pleased to give you credit for any uncut lumber you have left over — even undamaged windows or doors. When purchasing doors that are on sale, especially second-hand ones, look carefully to see if they are perfectly straight and are not warped. For exterior doors, the one and three-quarter inch, solid-core door is recommended. The solid-core is stronger than a hollow-core and is not so easily broken through by an intruder. The hollow-core door, one and three-eighth inch constructed of two pieces of thin wood sandwiching a thick solid wooded frame, is satisfactory for interior use.

If vinyl flooring is to be used over the floor deck, the pattern and coloring of the tiles should match perfectly from box to box. Cases have been known where the tile has been laid over most of the floor deck and when going back to buy more to finish the job, the boxes are of a different run and the tiles will not match.

For sloped roofing, asphalt shingles are usually used. You may want to use the self-sealing shingles which seal and keep the tabs down in the face of high winds. A flat built-up roof may cause difficulty even if done by a professional roofer; avoid it if possible.

If considerable concrete is used for piers, footings, or foundation walls, it may be desirable to have the cement already mixed with sand, gravel and water, delivered to your home ready for use. If minimum quantities are involved, however, a telephone call to a supplier will help determine if you should buy individually bagged Portland cement, gravel and sand from a builders' supply company, and a wheelbarrow from a hardware store.

Glass for the normal size window will come with the window units you purchase at the lumber yard. Plate glass for picture windows must be purchased from a glass company; by shopping around, you can save on this glass. Instead of the polished plate glass you may be able to use the cheaper heavy sheet glass, which presents a slight distortion due to a waviness in its structure.

The existing central heating plant can be used for heating the new room, but one must remember that heavy insulation of the ductwork or wrapping of the pipes will be required. Hot-air distribution pathways for both the hot air supplied to the room and the air returning to the furnace will also be necessary. Tapping on to your existing heating system should be done if possible, but also prepare for use of additional auxiliary heat to balance and supplement the central system. Often the new addition has large wall areas exposed to the weather.

If electric heating is used, the baseboard convector heater is usually preferable. One with thermostatic control is recommended. A heavy metal or water-filled heater (inhibited with ethylene glycol to prevent freezing), is desirable to smooth out abrupt and large changes in room air temperature which occur when the thermostat operates. Portable heaters of this nature are advertised often by local stores, but these units only deliver from 1300 to 1600 watts — not enough in a ten by fifteen foot room in twenty degree weather. Code requirements specify the depth which piers and their footings must be placed into the ground below the frost line and down to original undisturbed earth. Check with local authorities before making your estimate of the costs required for the spare room.

Patios. Many people who have bought a new house will desire to put in a new patio. Should you do this, avoid any monolithic flat structure, such as a concrete patio which will crack as the new ground settles. Instead, put in a patio floor consisting of flagstone or bricks laid in bluestone, dirt, or sand which may settle one at a time and will be easier to lift and reset. Above all wait for over a year until the dirt settles before you build a patio.

New siding. The use of pre-painted aluminum siding is an attractive possibility for covering old and battered siding. Original causes for peeling paint or rotting wood cannot be cured by this covering material. Consequently, the cure must be made before the aluminum covering is used. (For more information on aluminum siding see Chapter 3.) Vinyl siding is another possibility.

Renovating the kitchen. Renovation of a kitchen is usually done by a contractor. There are many unreliable people in this field, so make a thorough investigation before you sign a contract.

A useful publication for a homebuyer who plans to redo a kitchen can be purchased from the Small Homes Council, Building Research Council, University of Illinois at Urbana, Champaign, Illinois, 61801. Title of publication is Kitchen Planning Guide. Magazines about the home and garden often have good suggestions about remodeling. Consult your library.

It is suggested that when you write for the Kitchen Planning Guide, you also ask for Bibliography of Circulars, Technical Notes, Research Reports, Instruction Sheets and Special Publications. All of these are clear, well written, and helpful to househunters, homeowners, and builders.

II. A WORD ABOUT ENERGY SAVING

ADVANTAGES AND DISADVANTAGES OF THE VARIOUS FUELS

Which is the most expensive type of heating: gas, oil, or electricity? Electric heating is considerably more expensive because of transmission losses from the generating plant and the power lost in pushing electrons through the heating elements. However, in some areas of the U.S., such as in the Tennessee Valley, the kilowatt-hour cost of electricity is relatively low and electric heating competes with the other two types. Gas heating and oil heating costs were approximately the same until the recent oil shortage.

The high cost of electric heating is softened by other factors. As the electric companies say in their advertising, electric heating is clean heating. Since no flames are involved, the possibility of unburned gas or oil fumes is non-existent.

Unburned gas is a health hazard. In a hot-air gas-fueled furnace, cracks can eventually develop in the heat exchanger; this allows unburned gas which is destined for the chimney to seep into the hot-air circulation system. (See Chapter 6.)

Since the gas range is often operated without the exhaust fan turned on, there is always some unburned gas in the living quarters of the house. This occurs to a small degree as the three pilot lights burn day and night. Small amounts of gas, from cooking and burning of the pilot lights, can be offensive to some who have allergic tendencies.

Another advantage of electric heating is that any flame-heating increases the passage of outdoor air in and out of the house through the cracks in the structure. This factor is easily seen in a fireplace, where air to feed the flames comes through cracks under the windows and doors, provides oxygen for the flames, and exhausts through the chimney. Electric resistance heaters don't contribute significantly to the change of air in the house.

THE CONTRIBUTION OF
APPLIANCES TO HEATING

The energy used for the cooking range, water heater and miscellaneous appliances in a house makes some contribution towards warming the house in any season of the year. This auxiliary heating reduces the load on the heating system in cold weather and increases the load on the cooling system in hot weather.

In parts of the U.S. where air-conditioning is not used significantly, this extra source of heating can be an important and helpful net contribution. In southern areas, heavy appliance use can place a burden on the air-conditioner and the net gain will be small.

Heat loss from the jacket or chassis of a water heater to the surrounding air contributes significantly to heating. In 1958 to 1961, studies were made by the National Bureau of Standards of energy usage in Air Force houses at the Little Rock Air Force Base; they showed that the jacket loss of electric water heaters was eight to ten percent of the total monthly energy used for water heating. This means that an oversized heater in northern climates, such as a fifty gallon heater for two retired people, would not waste energy; in southern states, however, a thirty gallon heater would be better.

It is probable that the electric energy used by electric lights, resistance heaters, toasters, irons, and radio and television sets would be converted into heat. The situation with respect to clothes dryers is less definite; although there would be some heat transferred to the room from the jacket of the dryer, these devices are usually equipped with a small fan which uses room air to carry the water vapor and heat through a vent to the outdoors. In gas heaters, the unburned gas and other waste products from the flame, which contain heat, are also vented to the outdoors.

Many householders vent the hot water vapor from electric dryers to the inside of the basement or utility closet through a lint catcher. This is a saving in the winter months, but a vent is of course desirable in summer months; a special device for summer adaptation would serve the purpose. (See Chapter 5 describing a homemade device for this.)

FUTURE ENERGY-SAVING TECHNIQUES

With the sudden realization that our energy sources are limited, ways of harnessing the sun's energy are being developed and new gadgets are making their appearance. (See Chapter 6.) It would be wise for all prospective homebuyers to keep their eyes open for these developments.

Consider all the heat that escapes from a house during a day's operation — hot water down the drain, hot unburned gas up the chimney, heated air out through the cracks and openings in the walls, attic and roof, and heat itself through walls, ceilings, and windows. Stop and think about the heat that comes in during the summer — through cracks and openings with the air and by itself through the walls, attic and roof.

Utilization of waste heat. Utilization of waste heat is one profitable answer for energy saving. New methods will soon be marketed for recovering the heat going up the chimney from gas and oil-fueled hot-air furnaces or water heaters. Heat exchangers will use a stream of water or air in a metal conduit to nestle next to the hot flues and catch the heat. Devices will open dampers and operate fail-safe devices in the flue only when the flame is on. Heat exchangers will use the heat in the hot water going down the drain.

The Center for Building Technology at the National Bureau of Standards is presently experimenting with small-volume, gas-fired hot water heaters; these save fuel and may be as effective as the larger heaters. Some of these heaters employ finned heat-exchangers that pick up heat from the hot exhaust fumes and return it to the water being heated.

Elimination of pilot lights. Another possibility for saving is the use of electronic spark ignition in place of pilot flames. In the average home using gas, about 1000 BTU/hr of power is required for these flames. Only about 0.00020 BTU/hr would be required in the same house if electronic spark were used.

The future house

In spite of these problems, houses today do work well. Because modern construction methods employ storm windows or double-glazed windows, six inches of fiberglass insulation in the attic floors and four inches in walls, and because of the inevitable and accidental cracks that occur during construction, our homes are protected fairly well from heat loss and at the same time are adequately supplied with outdoor air for ventilation.

However, this can be improved. More and better insulation could be placed in the walls at reasonable cost, as well as tight sealing to close the openings that let in the outside air. This tight sealing when the family is large and there is lots of washing and cooking, can cause excessive moisture in a house.

A house-of-the-future with this superwall and tight sealing would be provided with automatically operated inlet and exhaust vents to let in air (or humidity) or to exhaust air (or humidity) when needed. Both temperature sensors and humidity sensors would be involved. The house might need a dehumidifier if it is small and there are many children. Heating and air-conditioning would be tied into the automatic system.

MAKING DO WITH THE
PRESENT HOUSES

Newspapers and utility companies have provided the public with copious and repetitive suggestions on how to save energy in our present houses. A number of suggestions were also presented in the preceding material of this book. It is surprising how much energy and money can be saved following these suggestions.

In a test performed in 1973 at the Bureau of Standards' Center for Building Technology, a house was insulated with six inches of fiberglass in the attic and three and one-half inches in the walls, and placed in a large chamber at minus two degrees; energy savings were about fifty-five percent compared to those for an uninsulated house. The house was heated by a gas-fired hot-air furnace and the temperature was maintained at seventy-three degrees. Heat losses for the uninsulated house without storm windows were not determined by testing but were calculated using mathematical techniques.

One of the largest sources of heat loss is by means of infiltration through cracks and openings. Table 4 below, gives a breakdown of heat loss for the test and shows this clearly both for cases with and without insulation. In both cases it amounted to about 10,000 BTU/hr, but the percentage of loss due to the infiltration factor differed for the two situations. For the insulated situation it was 36.5 percent and for the uninsulated case it was 16.4 percent.

TABLE 4
BREAKDOWN OF HEAT LOSS IN
TEST HOUSE

	With insulation		Without insulation	
	BTU/hr	(%)	BTU/hr	(%)
Through roof	3,100	11.0	16.700	27.4
Through walls	6,900	24.6	22,000	36.1
Through floors	1,000	3.6	5,600	9.1
Through doors	1,000	3.6	1,000	1.6
Through windows	5,800	20.7	5,700	9.4
By means of in-filtration thru cracks and openings	10,200	36.5	10,000	16.4
Total	28,000	100.0	61,000	100.0

This test shows both the importance of insulation and the need for minimizing air infiltration and caulking up cracks around windows and doors, especially if the house is heated by hot-air.

12. HOME INSURANCE POLICIES AND INSPECTION SERVICES

Warranties for New Homes. The Home Owners Warranty program began in 1973 under the administration of the Home Owners Warranty Corporation (HOW), a subsidiary Corporation of the National Association of Homebuilders (NAHB). This was the first step towards a successful program to protect the homebuyer; it is beneficial to both builder and buyer, and a credit mark to the building industry.

The new program was badly needed. Even though many sound and waterproof houses were built during the big housing boom of the 1950's, 1960's and early 1970's, the demand was often so great that some builders were not thorough; they cut corners and left the buyers with defective homes. Heavily-cracked foundations, caved-in backyards, carpets heavily worn after a year, inadequate heating systems, curled floor tiles, and jammed windows were not uncommon.

There were many cases of litigation, but the lawsuits brought little satisfaction to the injured buyer. Thousands of homebuyers were disenchanted, demoralized, and humilitated.

Although the NAHB plan with its promise of protection will help to diminishing the ill practices and public disenchantment, it has not had the benefits of time and experience; consequently one cannot yet say that the consumer has found full protection. Nonetheless, promise is there.

Under the plan the builder and the buyer sign a home

warranty agreement; the salesperson is not involved. The major points of the agreement are shown below.

- The program offers a ten year warranty to the buyer against major defects.
- During the first year, the builder covers defects caused by faulty workmanship and materials due to non-compliance with locally and nationally approved standards.
- During the first and second years, the builder is responsible for major construction defects and for defects in the installation of plumbing, heating, electrical, and cooling systems of the home; this does not include appliances, equipment, and fixtures which may or may not carry a manufacturer's warranty.
- From the third through the tenth year of the warranty, the insurance company* covers major construction defects only; it has no right of subrogation** against the builder. The insurance company also underwrites the builder's performance during the first two years of the builder's warranty responsibilities, if for any reason the builder fails to make good on his warranty obligation.
- In signing the home warranty agreement the buyer agrees to keep and maintain the home in good repair and condition, and to comply with warranty requirements of the manufacturers of equipment, appliances and fixtures.
- The home warranty agreement provides a process for resolving any dispute about a defect involving possible non-compliance with approved standards. Three aspects of the process are outlined below:

(1) In the first two years the buyer must deal directly with the builder and must put his complaint in writing. Local Warranty Councils, which are established to administer the program in specific geographical areas, are empowered to

---

*A company which issues insurance to HOW, the benefit of which is assigned to the homebuyer.
**To act to recover its expenditures from the builder.

resolve disputes which cannot be resolved between the buyer and builder. If the Local Warranty Council fails to resolve the complaint within thirty days after written notice requesting conciliation, then either builder or customer may ask the Local Council to arrange for the American Arbitration Association to resolve the problem. The insurer will honor any arbitrator's decision which the builder fails to honor, with respect to his obligations under the first two years of the warranty. However, during the first two years of coverage, the insurer has the right of subrogation against any builder failing to comply with the arbitrator's decision. The National HOW Corporation can suspend or expel from HOW any builder who fails to comply with an arbitrator's decision.

(2) In years three through ten the buyer can make a claim for major construction defects only. To do this, he must write to the Local Warranty Council directly (NOT to the builder). If the buyer is dissatisfied with the finding of the Local Warranty Council concerning his claim during these years, he may request arbitration of the matter.

The insurer will honor any arbitrator's decision during the third through the tenth year, with no right of subrogation against the builder. Additionally, the insurer will indemnify and defend the builder against any action brough against him.

It is possible that two weaknesses in the arbitration system may cause difficulty.

(a) The Warranty Council is composed of builder members, perhaps a one-sided jury, and (b), the interpretation of "major defects" is foggy and may not be in the best interest of the homeowner.

(3) Nominal deposit fees, some of which are refundable, are involved in the program for resolving disputes.

- The warranty and certificate which a buyer receives are transferrable to successive owners of the house within a ten-year period.
- The cost of the warranty is based, at the time of writing, on the following formula: $2 for every $1,000 of the final selling price of the home, or a total of 0.002 percent of the final

211

selling price of the house. For example, on a house which finally sells for $40,000, the cost for ten year coverage will be one $80 payment (a charge which is presumably included in the cost of the house).

The home warranty agreement defines a "major construction defect" as "actual damage to the load bearing portion of the house (including damage due to soil movement) which affects its load bearing function and which vitally affects or is imminently likely to produce a vital effect on the use of the house for residential purposes." Other specific definitions are included in the warranty agreement.

The program is voluntary, and some builders do not accept it. The buyer should ask the builder if he is a member of HOW. It is to the builder's advantage to belong because it gives him a clear selling advantage over non-participating builders. Also, he will in the future be able to enjoy the benefits of comprehensive records of defects — and corrective measures taken — accumulated over the nation by the program administrators.

The prospective buyer of a new home is advised to write the Home Owners Warranty Corporation, 15th and M Sts., Washington, D.C., 20005, for information about the new program.

Warranties for New and Resale Homes. The National Home Inspection Service, Inc. (NHIS) offers a Home Buyer's Protection Plan through which a buyer can make use of its home inspection service when considering a new or resale house. For an extra fee, NHIS, under their *Guarantee of Structural, Mechanical and Electrical Condition*, also guarantees the components of the house and property inspected by them. The guarantee applies for one year from the date of the inspection, with certain rights accruing to a new purchaser or to the original mortgagee of the property if the property is sold within a year.

Following is the schedule of components that apply.
1. The central heating system
2. The central cooling system
3. The plumbing system

212

4. The roofing
5. The electrical system
6. The structural soundness of the exterior and interior walls, ceilings and floors
7. The structural soundness of the foundation.
8. The basement, both as to structural soundness of the foundation and the absence of chronic water penetration.

A sheet showing details of the schedule of components is attached to the guarantee signed by the customer and authorizing officer of the Inspection Service Company. For example, under the component for *Basement* the following is stated: *"Basement masonry walls and concrete floors; water (not dampness) running down basement walls or draining across basement floor; sump pump."* Spaces are provided for exclusions under each listing of component details, to protect the Inspection Service Company from paying for defective items the customer accepted when the house was purchased.

1. A number of these items may be excluded if the condition or age raises doubts as to possible trouble.

2. A deductible sum, usually $100, is standard.

3. The policy covers *defects,* not degree of efficiency, and limits corrective action to whatever degree of repair is required; it does not necessarily cover replacements.

Another warranty service that has come into some prominence in the last two years is the Buyers Protection Plan sponsored by Electronic Reality Associates, Inc. This corporation has over 600 offices nation-wide, and by electronic means, offers the buyer rapid access to pictures and descriptions of houses for sale in any locality in the U.S. It conversely offers a service to the seller of a house, by seeking out people moving in from other parts of the country. Any qualified real estate brokerage firm can become a member organization.

The warranty is offered, for an extra charge, to buyers who purchase a house through the Electronic Realty Associates.

When title is taken to a house the buyer is issued a Buyer's Protection Plan Agreement with endorsement, entitling him or her to a 24-hour-a-day telephone number for repair service. The ERA Brochure states, "When anything covered breaks down, call them, toll free. They'll send a professional repairman to your door as fast as he can get there. You pay nothing for parts, labor, or anything else. Not for any call either. For *any call* for a full year." Since the plan is new, its full effectiveness has not been fully established.

Specifically covered by the Buyer's Protection Plan are:

1. The central heating system, or wall, floor or window heating units.
2. The plumbing fixtures except toilet seats.
3. The plumbing system contained within the home.
4. The electrical system within the home.
5. All types of water heaters.
6. All sheet metal duct work.
7. All central air conditioning systems, including window units less than five years old.
8. Built-in appliances which are fixtures.
9. Water softener system, except the salt and mineral beds.
10. Roofs (based on number of years in service).

As in the case of the National Home Inspection Service plan, detailed specifications for coverage, involved in each of the above ten items, are listed.

The Electronic Realty Associates specializes in resale houses. For further information write the Electronic Realty Associates, 8600 West 63rd Street, Shawnee Mission, Kansas 66201.

There are doubtless many other plans — some local in nature, and most of which offer one year guarantees. The homebuyer is urged to sign a contract only under the coverage of a good plan, the best of which to date appears to be the plan offered by the Home Owners Warranty Corporation.

HOME INSPECTION SERVICES

A valuable service which has made its appearance on the housing market in recent years is the House Inspection Service which is operated by organizations representing the prospective buyer. These organizations will inspect a house before the contract is signed or after the contract is signed to satisfy contingent clauses. A typical contract contingency might read: "Purchaser shall have the privilege of engaging a professional home inspection service to examine the mechanical and structural conditions of the property. Report must be satisfactory to purchaser or at purchaser's option all deposit monies shall be returned and obligations of the contract voided." Usually a time limit is stipulated.

When the inspector has completed the inspection, he will give the buyer a written list of defects or possible defects which may come about at a later date. A good report will point out positive assets as well. Comments usually include depreciation factors, design, maintenance difficulties, special problems, material and workmanship.

The pre-purchase home inspection service is becoming standard practice in some areas. This growth and demand for well-trained inspectors will undoubtedly lead to the entry of a few unqualified persons and unethical practices within the inspection services. Ask and check references and conflicting interests. The qualifications of the better inspectors will include a background of building experience and broad but technical formal high level training and education.

Avoid part-timers who may be otherwise engaged in contracting, real estate, or other conflicting interests.

13. IMPORTANT ITEMS YOU MAY MISS

Adequate closet space.

Determine if there is enough closet space in the bedrooms.

Sufficient electrical outlets.

In older houses, lack of enough outlets is a common deficiency.

Snow guards on roof.

Snow guards on a roof in geographical areas having heavy snowfall are useful in keeping the snow from sliding off the roof on to people or shrubs below.

Safety items.

Look carefully for loose boards in porch, loose railings, indoor and outdoor stairways without railings, incomplete electrical connections (even in a new house), and ungrounded casings of clotheswasher and dryer.

Water outlets.

Determine if there are water spigots both in the back and in the front of the house or at least in a position so water will be available for both front and back yards.

Cockroaches.

Cockroaches are present in the best of homes, particularly in row houses and town houses where they can migrate from the dirtier homes to the cleaner homes. Keep a sharp eye out for these pests when you inspect; they are hard to get rid of.

Television antenna.
A good television antenna will add appreciably to your comfort and satisfaction. If one is already installed, ask about reception on local VHF and UHF stations, and ask about efficiency of cable. If there is none, determine if one is planned for your neighborhood in the future.

Sound transmission in walls.
Check for sound transmission in walls, particularly through walls separating dwelling units in row houses and town houses. One way—but not always a feasible way— is to turn the volume way up on a television in either the houses you are inspecting or the one next door, then listen through the wall. This item would well be the difference between your being happy in your house or having to sell.

Concrete in sidewalk and stoops.
Look for evidence of deteriorating concrete such as browned discoloration, chipping, crumbling, or flaking at surface.

Cost of electric and gas bills.
Before moving into a new community, check the price of electricity and gas.

FURTHER RECOMMENDED READING

Obtainable at U.S. Government Printing Office, Washington, D.C., 20402:

1. **Department of Agriculture.** Handbook for the Home—a 400 page Yearbook of Agriculture which offers advice for people who live in a city apartment, suburban or country house.

2. **Department of Housing and Urban Development.** Miminum Property Standards—One and Two Family Dwellings. No. 4900.1. Written principally for architects, builders, inspectors, and home inspection services, this thick book can be valuable to the prospective buyer who wants to dig deep into the technical aspects of a house. Requirements listed are *minimum* for houses financed under FHA. Must be ordered; cannot be obtained over the counter.

3. **Department of Housing and Urban Development.** Minimum Property Standards—Multi-family Housing. No. 4910.1, 1973 Edition. A companion publication to No. 4900.1.

4. **Department of Commerce, National Bureau of Standards.**
   a. 7 Ways to Reduce Fuel Consumption in Household Heating through Energy Conservation.
   b. 11 Ways to Reduce Energy Consumption and Increase Comfort in Household Heating.
   c. Retrofitting Existing Housing for Energy Conservation: An Economic Analysis.

ACKNOWLEDGEMENTS

Some material written by the authors of this book has previously appeared in The Washington Post and is printed here with permission.

The following organizations allowed us the use of pictures or sketches appearing in their publications. Their use is appreciated.

American Society of Heating, Refrigerating and Air Conditioning Engineers; 345 E. 47th Street, N.Y., N.Y. 10007.

American Technical Society; 848 East Fifty-Eighth Street, Chicago, Illinois, 60637.

Consumers Union of United States; 256 Washington St. Mt. Vernon, New York, 10550.

Material in this book on locks and security was copyrighted in 1971 by Consumers Union of United States, Inc. Reprinted by permission from Consumer Reports. February 1971.
Material on indoor-outdoor carpeting was copyrighted in 1973 by Consumers Union of United States, Inc. Reprinted by permission from Consumer Reports, August 1973.

Lau Industries; 2027 Home Avenue, Dayton, Ohio, 45407.

National Environmental Systems Contractors Association; 1501 Wilson Boulevard, Arlington, Virginia, 22209.

National Forest Products Association; 1619 Massachusetts Ave., N.W., Washington, D.C., 20036.

National Institute of Real Estate Brokers (of the National Association of Realtors); 155 E. Superior St., Chicago, Illinois, 60611.

North American Housing Corporation; Rock Hall Road, Point of Rocks, Maryland, 21777.

Prentice-Hall, Inc.; Englewood Cliffs, New Jersey, 07632.

Sears, Roebuck and Co.; Sears Tower, Chicago, Illinois, 60684.

GLOSSARY

Aggregate
The stone, gravel, or sand used with cement in mixing concrete.

Air-conditioner
An apparatus used for cooling a house.

Air-gap
A device in which water runs in one direction by gravity through an air-gap. Prevents the back-up of sewage into a dishwasher in the event of sewer blockage. Usually located in the sink top or wall near dishwasher.

Amperage or electrical current
The number of amperes used in a house, in an electrical circuit, or by an appliance. Amperage will vary widely in a house during day and night, depending on consuming ability of appliances used.

Ampere (AMP)
A unit defining the rate of flow of electricity (a unit of current) over a period of time.

Asbestos cement shingle
Fireproof roof or siding material made of Portland cement and asbestos fiber.

Asphalt shingles
Shingles made of heavy paper (felt) saturated with hot liquid asphalt, and covered with fine rock granules. Very common. although shorter life than others.

Atmospheric pressure
Pressure exerted by the air in the atmosphere. Varies considerably with altitude, time, and geographical location. For measurement purposes in engineering, normal atmospheric pressure is considered 14.696 lb. per square inch, 29.92 inches of mercury (in. Hg.), or 760 millimeters of mercury (mm. Hg.). Inches or mm. of Hg. indicates how high a column of mercury will rise in an air-evacuated, hollow glass tube, closed at the top, and placed in open dish of mercury.

Available amperage

The amount of current which is available when all the appliances are operating simultaneously. Also governed by sizes of fuses, circuit breakers, and wire sizes gauged to expected use. Sometimes called **connected** load.

Awning window

A window whose sash swings outward and up. Usually stacked several sashes high. The sashes are about 1 ft. wide and are not to be confused with the smaller slatted "jalousie" window. A "Hopper" window is an awning window upside down.

Backfill

Excavated soil replaced against a foundation or behind a retaining wall after completion.

Baseboard

The board, 4 to 6 inches high, placed around the periphery of the room at floor level in the same plane as the wall plaster. Principally decorative but hides imperfections in the plaster behind it.

Baseboard convector

A heating convector placed next to a baseboard in a room. (See convector.)

Beamed ceiling

A ceiling with exposed timbers placed horizontally along its surface. The timbers may be load-bearing, or hollow and merely decorative.

Bifold doors

A set of two folding doors.

Bitumen

A generic name for bituminous materials. Can be asphalt or coal tar pitch.

Black top

A bituminous product containing aggregates. Used for driveways and streets. Its durability is dervied from a solid base of crushed stone. A good black top driveway would consist of 2-3 inches of stone, 2 inches of coarse base, and topping of smooth black top.

Blade size (of a fan)

The diameter of the fan blade area of travel.

Blower

A squirrel-cage device in a furnace or air-conditioning unit that serves as a fan to blow conditioned air through the duct work of a house.

Bluestone

A common type of crushed stone consisting of basaltic rock. All sizes. Stays in place better than rounded bank and river gravel.

B.O.C.A.

Standard abbreviation for Building Officials and Code Administration International Inc. The building code book published by the organization is one of the country's most widely adopted code references.

Branch circuit

One of the electrical circuits which branches out from the electric service panel.

Brick veneer

A brick facing laid against exterior walls of a frame structure. Usually there is an air space between the veneer and the sheathing of the exterior wall. The veneer does not support any weight of the building.

BTU

British thermal unit, a unit of heat; the amount of heat required to raise the temperature of one pound of water one degree Fahrenheit. The unit BTU/hr (BTUH) is a power unit (instead of a heat unit) and is used for quoting the capacity of heating or air-conditioning equipment. Its metric equivalent, a term encountered principally in electrical measurement, is the watt. One watt equals 3.142 BTU/hr, and as the U.S. goes metric it will be used for heating and air-conditioning capacity. The use of BTU/hr or watt for cooling equipment seems anomalous, but it implies heat removal and makes sense.

Bulkhead cabinet

Small kitchen cabinets placed above the regular wall cabinets. They are about a foot high and reach to the ceiling.

BX cable (armored cable)

A metal-clad, jointed, electrical cable suitable only for indoor use, unless of special type.

Capacity

A term used to describe the merit of a piece of apparatus; e.g., for a furnace or air-conditioner BTU per hour; for a ventilating fan cubic feet per minute (CFM) of free air delivery.. For a refrigerator or hot water tank, the term has a different connotation, meaning storage volume or water-holding capacity, respectively.

Cartridge fuse

A heavy-duty fuse shaped like a bullet cartridge, for use in electrical circuit containing dryers, clothes washers, and other heavy-duty appliances. Also used for main, back-up fusing.

Casement window

A vertically hung window that swings out horizontally on its hinges, similar to door action.

Catalytic self-cleaning oven

An oven which cleans by means of a special coating on the oven lining.

Caulk

To fill seams and joints with a flexible, durable substance to make them watertight and to reduce air-leakage into a house. As a noun, the material used to caulk.

223

Cement

For this book, the term cement means Portland cement, a powdered mixture of silica, lime and alumina mixed in proper proportions and then burned in a kiln. Portland cement was invented in 1824 by an Englishman who burned limestone and clay (alumina and silica) together and ground up the mixture into a fine powder. He called it Portland cement because, when hard, it resembled a type of building stone found in Portland Isle, England.

Centigrade

A temperature scale in which the freezing point of water is called 0 degrees and its boiling point 100 degrees at normal atmospheric pressure. (29.92 in. Hg. or 760 mm. Hg.)

CFM

An abbreviation for cubic feet per minute. Usually gives a measure of volume of air moved by an electric fan or blower in one minute. It can also be a measure of volume of liquid moving in a tube, pipe or conduit.

Cinder block

A block made of Portland cement, water and cinders or slag. See definition for concrete block.

Circuit (electrical)

Two electric lines supplying current to lights or appliances.

Circuit breaker (C/B)

An automatic switch used in a panel box that disconnects flow of electrical current whenever a circuit is overloaded.

Clapboard

A long board, beveled so that one edge is thicker than the other. Used as siding with one clapboard overlapping the other.

Clean out cap

In plumbing, a large cap in the interior sewer line with a hex nut. Used for cleaning out the main sewer line.

Coliform count

A count of the bacteria Escherichia Coli in water to determine the safety of a drinking water supply. These bacteria are normal inhabitants in the intestinal tract of all human beings, and for this reason it can be safely assumed that water containing them in large numbers is contaminated.

Collar ties

Horizontal light framing members used near the apex of a roof to tie the rafters together and stiffen the roof.

Colonial door

Doors of Colonial raised panel design. A typical and popular door has been the six panel Colonial.

Column

A pillar; round or square, a vertical shaft which supports a porch floor or floor at a load-bearing point. May be non-bearing for decoration.

Compressor
The heart of an air-conditioning or heat pump system. It forces the refrigerant to travel through the system and also changes the refrigerant vapor (or gas) to a liquid, a process that gives off heat.

Concrete
The finished or hardened product after a mixture of cement, sand, gravel, and water has fully dried.

Concrete block
A building block made of Portland cement and water together with any type of aggregate. A common block would be about 8 x 8 x 16 inches in size, and may have hollow cavities open at top and bottom; usually has a cement-gray appearance, but comes in many other shapes, sizes, and colors. Cinder block is lighter than concrete block and is preferred by most builders for foundation work.

Condensate
The water resulting from condensation. In steam heating, it is water condensed from steam when it cools. In air-conditioning, it is the water that drips off the cooling coils into a drip pan and out to a drain point through a condensate line.

Condensation
Denotes a process in which water vapor (a gas) is changed to liquid water. Can also occur during vapor-liquid changes for liquids other than water; e.g., in a refrigerant.

Condenser
The outdoor unit of a central air-conditioning system which houses the compressor and other components. Its function is to cool the hot refrigerant vapor that comes from indoors and to compress it to a liquid at a slightly lower temperature. During the process, heat transferred from indoors is exhausted to the outdoors. A window air-conditioner has a self contained condenser that throws the hot air outdoors. Condenser in a heat pump is indoors during the winter and outdoors during the summer.

Conduit
A metal pipe covering electric wires.

Convector
A heating device designed to heat air which, in turn, heats a room by convection or a movement of air.

Conventionally-built house
A house which is constructed on the site by different workers of varying skills. Called a "stick-built" house.

Coolant
A medium for transferring "cooling" from one place to another. Usually liquid.

225

C.O.P.

Coefficient of performance of an air-conditioner or heat pump. A measure of energy output with respect to energy input. For electric conditioners or heat pumps the energy input from the utility lines is converted from units of electricity such as watt-hours to BTU. Seasonal C.O.P. is that C.O.P. occuring on the average for the entire season.

Chord

A structural member in a truss, such as the upper and lower chord. It can be made of any material.

Cornice

Projection at the top of a wall; a term applied to construction members under and around the eaves.

Course

A continuous and level row of shingles on a roof, or bricks or stones within the face of a masonry wall.

Crawl space

A space underneath a house or flooring. Usually two to three feet space for crawling; not a full height basement. A space behind a closet underneath a sloping roof.

Dead bolt

In a lock, the non-beveled, rectangular bolt in a lock mechanism.

Dew point temperature

That temperature at which water condenses out of air and at which the relative humidity of the air is 100 percent. Varies, depending on the amount of moisture in the air and on the air pressure.

Diffuser

A vent. A round device placed in a ceiling with annular openings from which conditioned air passes into the room below. Usually used for cooling system. Purpose similar to a register.

Dormer

A projection from a sloped roof designed to increase habitable space below this roof. A vertical window provided at the end of the projection is known as a dormer window.

Double-hung window

A window that opens and closes by raising and lowering. One with an upper and lower sash, balanced by sash cords and weights or a spring and friction counter balance.

Double-keyed lock

A door lock that has two keyways, one that locks the door from the outside and the other that locks it from inside. Purpose is to preclude an intruder from breaking a pane of glass, reaching in, turning a knob and opening the door.

Downspout

A metal pipe extending from the roof gutter to the ground to carry off rainwater. Also called a leader.

Dry-bulb temperature (DBT)

Temperature indicated on a normal glass thermometer or temperature-indicating device. Term used in contrast to wet-bulb temperature. (See definition of wet-bulb temperature.)

Dry rot

A disintegration of wood caused by fungi growing in moist sections of the wood. Actually dry rot is a misnomer.

Dry-stone wall

A retaining wall made of stones and rubble which are not joined with mortar.

Drywall

Wall in a building composed of panels of prefabricated plaster. A panel consisting of gypsum plaster covered on both sides with thick sheets of paper. Called Sheetrock, a trade name, by builders and carpenters. Also known as plaster board.

Dry-well

A gravel or stone-filled hole in the soil to catch water run-off from the roof or floor areas. Often used instead of a drain in a stairwell leading to a basement.

Ducts

Pipes with relatively large cross-sectional areas for delivering conditioned air to a living space or returning it to a heating or cooling device. Also used to carry exhaust fumes from kitchen and bath fan to the outdoors.

Eave

The area near the lower angle of the roof and the outside wall. May refer to either inside or outside.

Effluent

An outflow of liquid or gas.

Electric service panel

A metal cabinet housing the main service switch and circuit-breakers or fuses. From this cabinet wires branch out to the different parts of the house. Known as panel box or service panel.

Electronic air filter

An air filter which collects dust and other particulate matter by means of electrically charged plates.

Elephant trunk

Round, flexible duct.

Eutectic salt

Certain eutectic salts used in solar heating systems store a large amount of heat in latent form. This can be used later when the salts cool and

227

change from liquid to solid form. The term **eutectic** means "melts easily."

Evaporative cooler

A cooling device, used in relatively dry geographical areas, which employs the principle of evaporating water.

Evaporator

The indoor unit of an air-conditioning system; installed indoors in the plenum of a furnace, or in a separate chassis of its own. The trades refer to it as the "A" coil because of the shape of the coil layout. Its function is to cause the liquid coming from the condenser outdoors to be expanded suddenly into a gas, thereby causing an evaporation and cooling effect. The expanded gas travels through the copper coils of the evaporator over which house air passes to be cooled. The cool air then goes on its way through the ducts to the rooms of the house. A window air-conditioner also has an evaporator. Evaporator in a heat pump is outdoors during the winter and indoors during the summer. When the evaporator is not used in conjunction with an existing furnace and fan unit, but within a chassis of its own, it is often referred to as an air handler.

Expansion tank

A tank used in hydronic heating system; purpose is to allow for expansion of water when it is heated.

Eye beam

A steel structural beam. In a house it is used slightly below ceiling level in a basement to support a load bearing partition. Looking at it endwise, it presents the shape of the letter "I".

Fahrenheit

A temperature scale in which, under normal atmospheric pressure (29.92 inches of Hg. or 760 mm. of Hg.) 32 degrees denotes freezing and 212 degrees the boiling point of water. The scale was invented by Gabriel Fahrenheit in 1714.

Family room

A room where the family gathers. Often has a fireplace; less formal than a living room.

Fibrous insulation.

House insulation having a loose quality like a blanket, as opposed to solid, block-like insulation. Glass fiber insulation which comes in blankets or batts is the most common of the type. Purpose of fibrous insulation is to inhibit heat flow by conduction.

Fiberglass

The same material as glass fiber. The terms are used interchangeably. See Fibrous Insulation.

Fin

A thin and rectangular or square piece of metal fastened perpendicularly to a pipe which carries a hot liquid for heating, or cool liquid for cooling. A line of fins is placed on the principal pipe of a baseboard convector, or on the cooling coils of an air-conditioner.

Finish coat
Final coat of paint applied over primer, primer-seal or other type of undercoat.

Firestop
Incombustible material used to stop the spread of fire between sections of a building. Also, wood blocks placed horizontally between studs to reduce draft or flue action during a fire.

Fire wall
A wall made of incombustible material between adjacent living quarters to prevent the spread of fire through a building.

Flashing
Sheet metal or other material used around chimneys, projecting pipes, or in roof valleys to protect a structure from water leakage.

Flue
An enclosed passageway, such as a pipe or chimney, for carrying off smoke, gases, or air.

Flush contemporary door
A smooth surface door with no moldings or raised panels. Much in use today.

Foamed plastics
Plastics which have been foamed or extruded in the manufacturing process. Are very nearly impervious to water, have excellent insulating properties and high R-designation; have the disadvantage of being somewhat combustible even though treated by the manufacturer to inhibit flame spread. Two most common foamed plastics are foamed polystyrene and polyurethane which are usually marketed for insulation in houses in board form (rigid insulation). (See R-designation in Glossary.)

Footing
An enlargement at the bottom of a wall or column for the purpose of spreading the weight of the column or wall over a large surface area. Sometimes called a footer. It usually extends down into the ground below frost level.

Foundation
The part of the wall on which the building is supported, synonomous with basement wall when the house has a basement. In some geographical areas footing and foundation are used interchangeably.

Foyer
An inside entrance hall.

Framing or frame
The lumber work which makes up the various structural parts; the

229

woodwork of doors, windows, trusses and other structural members; the entire lumber work supporting the floors, walls, roof, and partitions.

French drain

A drainage system composed of loose and porous material. Often with a drain tile open-joint pipe. Used to carry off or collect excess water.

Furring

A process of providing a nailing surface and a space between indoor wall finish and the main structural wall of masonry. Space is provided with use of furring strips of flat, narrow, pieces of lumber. Often placed 16 inches apart. Any partition may be furred out to make it wider.

Furring strips

Strips of wood used behind an indoor wall covering to provide space between that wall and the exterior wall. Used also between a false wall and an interior wall.

Gable

The vertical triangular section of wall formed by two converging roof lines.

Grade

The ground level around a building.

Ground

A reference point at which electric potential is zero; any metal structure that goes into the ground which has an electric potential of zero; a ground wire from the panel box to the earth. Ground would offer no danger if touched.

Grounding

An electrical term. Denotes connecting a wire from the metal casing or chassis of an appliance directly to the earth under a building or to a metal element, such as a water pipe, that is electrically connected to the ground.

Gutter

A trough or open channel made of metal, plastic, or wood, installed along the bottom of a sloping roof to collect and carry off rain water.

O.G. Gutter

Fig. 44.

Half-round gutter

Fig. 45.

Box gutter

Fig. 46.

Gutter guards

A wire screen placed over a gutter to prevent it from collecting leaves.

Gypsum

A native rock composed of calcium sulfate crystallized with about 20 percent water. Calcined gypsum is used in plaster.

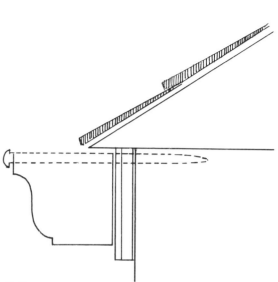

Fig. 44. O.G. Gutter.

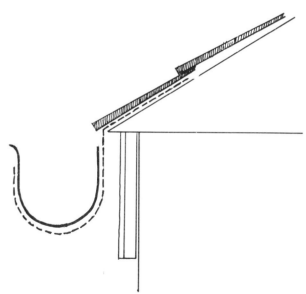

Fig. 45. Half-round gutter.

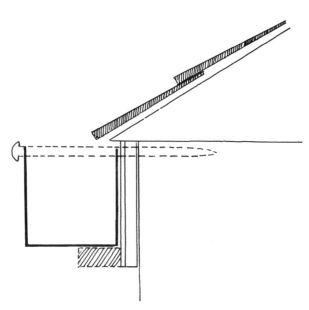

Fig. 46. Box gutter.

Gypsum board
See drywall
Header
A wood framing member that receives supporting load from joists, rafters or studs, and transfers the weight to other places. Similar to a beam, but built flush into the framing members, not below as when heading off for a stairway or hearth opening. In a building, a brick or stone laid with its end toward the face of the wall. It is the tie-course that secures the facing with the backing material.
Hearth
The floor of a fireplace; also the portion of the floor immediately in front of the fireplace.
Heat exchanger
A device by which heat is exchanged from one heat-carrying medium to another without contact between the two media.
Heat gain
An increase in the amount of heat in a space within a building, or in a structural element such as a glass in a window. English unit of measurement in a building or air space is BTU/hr. In a structural element it is measured in BTU/hr. per sq. foot of that element.

232

Heat pump

An apparatus similar to a central air-conditioner, but with some auxiliary parts, used for heating in the winter and cooling in the summer.

Hip

The apex of two intersecting upward converging roof lines, Opposite of a roof valley.

Hip roof

A roof which rises by inclined planes from all four sides of the building. Eliminates the gables.

Hollow-core door

A door constructed of two pieces of thin wood sandwiching a solid, outer wood frame. Door is hollow in the center, with cardboard reinforcing.

Humidifer

A device, either portable or attached to a furnace, that provides moisture to the air in living quarters. Four principal types are: (1) Plate type; small plates, about four by six inches and made of a fibrous material, are wetted by capillary action from water in a reservoir and generate moisture in the air by evaporation; (2) Rotating drum type: a drum having a fibrous media around its circumference which rotates slowly in a reservoir so that water droplets form on the media and are blown into the hot-air stream by a small auxilliary fan. A rotating disc type made up of a metal meshwork works on the same principal; (3) Wet-pad; water cascades slowly over a metal or fibrous media so that droplets are formed and moisture is blown into the air-stream by an auxiliary fan; and (4) Atomized type; the water atomized by centrifugal action or by a nozzle, which blows the water directly into the air-stream.

Humidistat

A device which automatically senses and controls humidity in a living space. Controls the action of a humidifier.

Humidity

A general term denoting the amount of water vapor in the air. Can be absolute humidity which describes the actual amount of water in the air, or relative humidity. (See relative humidity.)

Icedam

A dam or ridge of ice formed at the cold, lower extremities of a roof. This dam causes the melting ice flowing down from the warmer part of the roof to back up under shingles and to flow down into and damage the inner structural members of the house.

Insulated windows

Windows with two panels, separated one from another by a cushion of air, to reduce heat transmission. Often called double-glazed windows.

Jalousies
Aluminum framed windows with rows of opening glass stacked one above the other. They open simultaneously with a crank and resemble a venting louver or venetian blind. Used as a prime window in the south and for remodeling.

Jamb
The upright wood piece forming the side of a door or window opening.

Joists
Boards placed on edge which support walls, floors, and ceiling. Conventionally seen as 2 by 8's or 2 by 10's.

Junction box
A metal box which contains electrical junctions. Can be behind a wall switch, wall receptacle, or separately placed on a joist or other wood frame member. Inhibits fire spread when a short circuit develops within itself.

Keeper
A part of a door-lock system. The hole in the door jamb and lock plate into which a latch or bolt fits.

Kilowatt-hour
A thousand watt-hours. A unit used by utility companies for billing amount of power supplied to a customer over a period of time.

Latex paint
A water emulsion paint (an emulsion is a suspension of a liquid in a liquid, such as oil and water). Latex paints can be of various types and are particularly useful for porous, absorbent surfaces, such as plaster and masonry. The term latex is misleading; the paint has no relation to latex rubber.

Lath
A backing for a plaster wall. A material fastened to studs or to masonry, either directly or by means of furring strips, made so that plaster adheres to it. Three kinds of lath have been used — wood, metallic, and a gypsum plaster board. Metallic laths may be further subdivided into three classes: (1) A perforated sheet metal, (2) expanded metal, made by cutting slots in sheets, and (3) woven, chicken-wire type.

Leaching area
A large absorbent drain field or pit into which the liquid discharge of septic systems is returned to the earth.

Lead pan
A large sheet of lead placed under tile shower bases to make the base waterproof.

Load-bearing walls
A wall or partition which assists in bearing the load of floors and roof.

Lock plate
In a lock, the flat, metal plate which lies flush to the door jamb and

contains holes for bolts and latches in the locking mechanism. A keeper or striker plate.

Louver

An opening for ventilating closed attics or other spaces in a house; openings in a diffuser or register. When used for attic ventilation, it allows air movement but is slatted to keep out rain. Should be screened to keep out animals.

L. P. gas

Liquid propane gas; shipped in liquid form to save space. It vaporizes on release of pressure and is made ready for fueling of cooking stoves and small heating appliances.

Masonry

Masonry material in the building trades are brick, concrete blocks, structural clay tiles, and stone. In some areas, cement, stucco and plaster are also classifed as masonry.

Master bedroom

A bedroom designed for the man and wife. Usually larger than childrens' rooms and guest rooms.

Mastic

A number of glue like materials used for securing floor coverings, drywall, wood panels, ceramic tile, and even structural components.

Media

A fibrous type of organic material or metal meshwork; used in evaporative coolers on which water drips, and which is cooled when evaporation of the water occurs. Also used to describe the material that catches lint or particulate matter in an air filter. Material that picks up water in a humidifier.

Methylene chloride

A chemical base in some paint removers. Slightly toxic; fumes in confined spaces should be avoided. Minimize breathing of fumes in open spaces.

Metric system

A rational system of weights and measures with decimal relationships between the units of measurement. Following are conversion factors for converting units from the older English system to the metric system.

Mineral wool insulation

Material used for insulating buildings; includes glass fiber (glass wool) and slagwool. Comes loose, or in blankets or batts.

Modular house

A prefabricated house which is shipped to the building site in large sections or modules.

Mortise lock

A lock system with (1) a dead bolt, a non-beveled, square-edged, tongue-like device, and (2) a convenience latch, a beveled latch that operates by the knobs inside and out.

Mullion

A window sash framing-member that separates 2 connected sashes (or windows).

Muntin

Small strip of wood or metal which separates the glass panes in a window.

Nail-popping

A condition occuring on drywalls where the heads of nails stick out.

Oil-base paint

Paint having oil as a binder or film forming base.

Pane

The glass section in a window.

Parging

A coat of cement applied to a masonry wall. Prevents foundation and basement walls from leaking.

Multiply these English units	by	to obtain these metric units.
inches	2.54	centimeters
feet	30.48	centimeters
yards	0.914	meters
miles	1.609	kilometers
sq. inches	6.452	sq. centimeters
sq. feet	0.09290	sq. meters
sq. yards	0.8361	sq. meters
ounces	28.35	grams
pounds	453.6	grams
fluid ounces	0.02957	liters
pints	0.4732	liters
quarts	0.9463	liters
gallons	3.785	liters
BTU	251.996	calories
BTU/hr.	.2931	watts
inches of mercury (pressure unit)	25.4	millimeters of mercury

To convert from Fahrenheit to centigrade (Celsius) the following equation should be used:

$$C = 5/9 \ (F \text{ minus } 32)$$

236

Parquet floor
A floor made of small blocks or squares of hardwood flooring; laid together with tongue and groove edges and secured to a base or subfloor with mastic or staples.

Partition
An interior wall separating one portion of a house from another.

Percolation
The process of a soil absorbing fluid. Septic systems for sewage disposal depend on good percolation.

Percolation test
In soil, tests whether water seepage into the ground is adequate for a septic system method of sewage disposal.

Perimeter insulation
Insulation, often of a rigid type, secured to the inside walls of crawl spaces. Also laid on the ground under the slab in slab-constructed houses.

Pier
A pillar or column supporting a structure, such as a house or room over a crawl space; a masonry structure used as an auxiliary to stiffen a wall.

Pile
That part of a carpet or rug made up of soft material; attached to the backing of coarse material.

Pile runners
A type of weather stripping on sliding windows or doors.

Pilling
The process of forming small globular masses of material in the carpet pile. This is not desirable, but develops with use.

Pitch
The slope of a roof expressed in a ratio of vertical rise to horizontal run, such as a 1:4, meaning the roof will rise 1 foot for every 4 foot of span. A 1:4 pitch would be flatter than a steeper 1:2 span. This ratio is often expressed with a base unit of span; for example, a 3:12 pitch.

Plaster
Any pasty type material of a mortar-like consistency used for covering walls or ceilings of buildings; hardens with time. Can also mean plaster board or drywall.

Plaster board
A rigid insulating board used in drywall construction. Made of plastering material, usually gypsum, covered on both sides by heavy paper.

Plate
The top or bottom horizontal member of a frame partition. A bearing plate of 2 inch thick lumber bolted to the top of a masonry wall to receive frame walls or joists.

Plenum

The collecting and mixing chamber over a furnace in the supply line, from which the conditioned air flows through ducts to the house. It is the metal ductwork box immediately above the furnace. In heating practice, it is often called the bonnet. When an air-conditioning system is in a house, the evaporator can be installed in the plenum so that cool air can be blown through the ductwork.

Polyvinyl acetate paint (PVA)

A paint of the latex type with excellent sealing qualities. Used often as a primer sealer.

Ponding

Denotes an accumulation of rain water in depressions of a flat roof, particularly an aspahlt or coal tar built-up roof.

Potable water

Water fit to drink.

Power pack

An assembly of electronic components which generates the high voltage charge on the plates of an electronic air filter.

Prefabricated house

A house in which many elements, such as trusses, rafters, joists, studs, and flooring elements, are fabricated into components or modules in a factory, and then shipped to a site for assembly and erection; eliminates much on-site labor and time.

Pre-filter

A fibrous filter placed ahead of the charged plates of an electronic air filter.

Primer

An undercoat, or preparation for the final coat of paint.

Primer sealer

In painting, a primer, or undercoat, used for sealing the surface so the material being painted will not suck in the final coat. Often called a sealant.

Pyrolytic self-cleaning ovens

Ovens which clean themselves with high heat.

R-designation

A designation for insulation, regardless of thickness, density or material, denoting its resistance to heat flow. Such designation is much more descriptive of the actual resistance property of the material than just thickness. For example, fiberglass insulation on the market through the years has decreased in density, and as a result a 6-inch thick blanket of the material 20 years ago would have had more resistance to heat flow than 6-inch thick material today. The R-designation was instituted in about 1970 and will not appear on insulation in older houses.

For the same thickness of fiberglass and rigid foamed plastic the R value is much different.

For present-day fiberglass insulation the relationship between the designation and thickness is as follows:

R-Designation	Approximate Thickness
R - 5	1 1/2 inches
R - 7	2 1/4 inches
R - 11	3 1/2 inches
R - 13	3 5/8 inches
R - 19	6 inches
R - 22	6 1/2 inches

For present-day foamed plastic insulation the relationship is as follows:

Foamed polystyrene

Approximate R-Value	Thickness
R - 5*	1 inch +

Polyurethane

R - 6**	1 inch -

Note the improved resistance to heat flow exhibited by these two foam products over the fiberglass material.

*Value quoted by Dow Chemical Co. for their product **Styrofoam**.
Value quoted by Dow Chemical Co. for their products **Thurane or **Zer-o-cell**.

Rafter
One of a series of sloping boards used in framing and for supporting roof loads.

Receptacle
An electrical device in a wall for receiving and making connections with a male plug connected to a lead cord of an appliance. An electrical outlet.

Recovery rate
A performance figure for hot water heaters, denoting how fast the temperature of a tank of water will recover after heavy usage.

Reflective insulation
A shiny aluminum sheet which reflects radiant heat.
Refrigerant
A chemical liquid used in an air-conditioner or heat pump to transfer heat from inside the house to the outdoors where it is exhausted. The refrigerant becomes a gas in one section of the system and is converted back to a liquid by the compressor. Used in heat pumps to transfer heat into the house during winter.
Register
A grille connected to a duct that directs hot air in winter and cold air in summer to pass into different rooms.
Reinforced concrete
Concrete which has been strengthened by reinforcing bars embedded in it.
Reinforcing bars
Steel or iron, deformed rods with ribs of projections along their length to offer reinforcement and added strength to concrete.
Relative humidity
A measurement of the amount of moisture in the air; the ratio of moisture the air holds to the amount it can hold at the same temperature and pressure. Expressed in percentage (i.e., the ratio in decimal form times 100). Example: 0.6 or 60%.
Reservoir
A small tank which holds water for use by a humidifier. Automatically fed at intervals by the hose water supply, it is nearly full of water at all times.
Resilient floor
Floors covered with materials such as vinyl and asphalt tile, or sheet goods such as linoleum.
Retaining wall
A masonry wall that holds back dirt fill. Sometimes constructed of wood, such as treated railroad ties.
Return duct
Duct in which air is returned to the furnace or evaporator of central air-conditioning system.
Ridge
The top of the roof at the apex (the extreme distance from the eave line).
Ridge vent
An elongated cap extending the entire ridge length to allow for attic ventilation. Its cross sectional view is shaped like a mushroom.
Rigid insulation
Insulation that comes in rectangular blocks and sheets which can be mounted between the studs, glued to walls or laid on the ground next to

concrete slabs. Two common types are foamed polystyrene and polyurethane. The former term is often called Styrofoam (a tradename).

Roof coating

A bituminous material with the consistency of pea soup; used for patching and waterproofing roofs, or filling voids in gutters.

Roof deck

The flat wood surface over which roofing material is placed.

Roofing cement

A bituminous material with a putty-like consistency, used for patching or waterproofing roofs. Contains asbestos fibers.

Service entrance cable

A heavy pair of insulated wires, or a conduit containing wires, through which electricity is provided to a house.

Service panel

Metal box with fuses or circuit breakers.

Shakes

A thick hand-split, rough-textured wood shingle.

Sheathing

A covering of cheap grade wood or fibrous sub-siding material nailed to exterior studs or rafters, sometimes referred to as subsiding; forms the base for finish operations.

Short circuit

A situation in which an electrical circuit has been crossed between an appliance and the service panel by a conducting element, so that much greater flow of current occurs than would normally occur when the appliance is in use. When a house is properly protected, the short circuit and high current flow will blow a fuse or cause a circuit breaker to operate; when not protected, can cause a fire.

Showerhead

A mechanism for producing the spray in a shower.

Shower pan

The base, or pan, for catching water under a shower stall.

Siding

The outer covering of a frame house; can be clapboard, plywood, aluminum, shingle, vinyl, or other protective material. In the trade, sometimes used synonomously with clapboards.

Sill plate

The bottom horizontal member of a frame partition. The wood bearing plate bolted to a masonry wall is sometimes called a sill plate.

Six panel door

See Colonial door.

Skim coat

A light, smooth, uniform, and finely troweled coat of gypsum topping mix over drywall.

Slab-on-ground

A concrete slab laid over the footings which supports a house without a basement. Any concrete slab poured on the ground, such as a porch or patio slab, with or without footings.

Sliding doors

Doors that slide horizontally on rollers on tracks.

Snow guard

Small protuberances on a roof; located close to and above the eaves to keep snow from sliding in sudden avalanches to the ground.

Solar heat gain

Heat gain on a wall, roof, or piece of glass, generated by radiant heat from the sun.

Solid brick construction

A house construction with brick walls built several courses thick to support the weight of the entire structure. Usually 8 to 12 inches thick. A brick house backed with masonry blocks is usually referred to as a solid brick house.

Solid core door

A door made of solid wood.

Spackle

Material used for patching drywall and wet plaster walls.

Spigot

A faucet or cock for controlling the flow of water out of a pipe.

Splash block

A thin rectangular masonry block with a trough on its top surface; laid on the ground to receive drainage water from a downspout (or leader) and carry it away from the building. Now being made of plastic.

Square of shingles

One hundred square feet of applied roof area.

Stack vent

In plumbing, a vertical vent pipe protruding through the roof to carry away sewer gas from the plumbing system, and to prevent a siphoning of traps by drawing air into the pipe system.

Stoop

A small porch. A raised platform with steps at the entrance of a house.

Structural clay title

A term applied to various sizes and kinds of hollow building units molded from surface clay, shale, fire clay, or a mixture of these materials. Used to back up brick or as a base for stucco.

Stucco

An exterior finish usually consisting of Portland cement, lime and sand. May contain gravel for rough texture.

Stud

A vertical length of lumber used to form a framework of a wall or partition. Nominally has a dimension of 2 by 4 inches, by 8 ft. long, but smaller dimensions are being used in houses of inferior construction.

Subfloor
A rough flooring laid over joists; provides a base for finish flooring.

Sump
A pit or depression where water is allowed to accumulate.

Sump pump
An apparatus used for siphoning water from a hole. Used in basement floors, particularly those below water-table level as a means for keeping the basement dry.

Supply duct
Duct which supplies conditioned air from furnace, central air-conditioner, or heat pump system, to rooms of a house.

Terrain
A general term used to describe the hills, ground level, trees and other natural parts of territory surrounding a house.

Therm
A term used in gas heating denoting a quantity of heat equivalent to 100,000 BTU.

Thermostat
A device for sensing and controlling temperature for a number of purposes in furnaces, hot water heaters, air-conditioners, heat pumps, and rooms. A thermostat installed on the wall of a room is known as a room thermostat.

Ton of air-conditioning
The removal of 12,000 BTU of heat per hour from the air. Origin of this unit occurred in the early days of the refrigeration industry when tests showed that 12,000 BTU per hour were required to melt one ton of ice.

Topping mixture
The final coat of gypsum applied over drywall joints. Smooth consistency and easy to work with sandpaper.

Trap
In plumbing, the trap in the sewer line to prevent sewer gas from seeping into the house without interrupting the flow of sewage. Visible under sinks in the shape of an "S".

Trigger bolt
A half-round cylinder next to the beveled latch in a lock; prevents an intruder from slipping a celluloid cord between the door jamb and the beveled latch so he can push the latch inwards and open the door.

Truss
A combination of members such as beams, bars, ties, and cords; usually arranged in triangular units to form a rigid framework for supporting a roof.

Underlayment

A non-structural rigid padding installed over subflooring to provide a smooth base for resilient floor. Some subfloorings incorporate smooth, finished surface with tongue-and-groove joints that eliminate the need for underlayment.

Valley

In architecture, a term applied to a depressed angle formed by the meeting at the bottom of two inclined sides of a roof. Opposite of hip.

Vapor barrier

A waterproof material placed on the warm side of insulation to prevent moisture from the living quarters from migrating to the insulation. Also can be of a non-permeable material such as a plastic sheet placed over a gravel bed underneath a concrete slab (for slab-on-grade construction) to prevent moisture from migrating from the dirt underneath, or material around, cold ducts or pipes to prevent "sweating" or moisture condensation in summer.

Ventilation

A process, involving the movement of air, for cooling air or driving moist air from a space in a building.

Vertical-bolt lock

A lock with two round bolts that go through two holes in its nesting plate. A good auxiliary lock.

Vibration isolator

A device for isolating vibration of a rotating piece of machinery from its surroundings.

Volt and voltage

An electrical unit defining potential for doing motor work or heating. It defines what is there and available for use. Assuming that the utility lines and transformer on the pole outdoors deliver a constant voltage to a house (which it doesn't), the voltage at the service entrance cable will remain approximately constant regardless of the appliances used in a house. This situation is entirely different from that which occurs for amperage or current which varies widely during the day and night, depending on the consuming ability of the appliances used.

Voltage drop

A drop in voltage occuring in a length of wire. The longer the length of the metallic wire and the smaller the diameter, the greater the voltage drop.

Watt

A metric unit of power, or heat per unit of time. Its English or engineering equivalent is BTU per hour. (For exact relationship between the two units see metric system.)

Watt hour

A unit of energy; power over a period of one hour.

Weephole

A small opening in a wall, such as a retaining wall, to allow drainage of excess water. Weep holes are used in brick veneer construction.

Wet-bulb temperature (WBT)

The temperature indicated on a glass thermometer covered with wet, wicking material. Because of the evaporation effect of the wet material, which depends on humidity of the air, this temperature will be lower than that indicated on a dry-bulb thermometer placed in an air space having the same atmospheric and temperature condition. A combination of the DBT and WBT provides information from which relative humidity of the air space can be determined. (See definition of dry-bulb temperature.)

Window-keyed lock

A lock that requires a key to open a window. Purpose is to prevent an intruder from breaking a pane of glass, reaching in, turning the window lock and opening the window.

Window sash

A movable part of a window contained in a window frame. The sash may consist of one pane of glass or many small panes; it may slide up and down, or in and out.

Wood framing

The timber work supporting the various structural parts of a house such as floors, walls, doors, windows, roofs and partitions.

INDEX

248